# Praise for *Surfing for God*

"This is a dangerous and beautiful book, filled with courage, filled with hope. This book will set you free. The process Michael describes here *works*—I've seen it happen with many men. That's why you should read this book. Then give it to every man you know."

—JOHN ELDREDGE
Author of *Wild at Heart* and *Beautiful Outlaw*

"*Surfing for God* is a miraculous book. A former hostage to pornography and its attendant evils, respected spiritual director Michael John Cusick shines a light on the dignity of our sexual desires, then points us to an open window through which he has led many men to freedom. Cusick explains the addict's situation clearly, placing it within its proper biblical context and summarizing the latest scientific research. He shows us that the dilemma is a spiritual one, rooted in our own disowned longings, especially our longing for God. He then delivers priceless practical direction. Any Christian concerned about the destructive effects of pornography on the contemporary church should read this book."

—NATE LARKIN
Founder of the Samson Society, Author of *Samson and the
Pirate Monks: Calling Men to Authentic Brotherhood*

"Michael Cusick has written a book where every page has at least one sentence that makes you understand this is not just 'everyman's battle' but a struggle that God has allowed so that we may really know that we cannot save ourselves—we need God. This book is rich with personal experience and professional guidance. It is a book about the wonderful mess of being sexual beings and not knowing how to live that out in the amazing way God intended. But after reading this, there is more hope, less shame, and greater freedom in imagining the dream God has for all of us."

—SHARON A. HERSH, M.A., L.P.C.
Author of *Begin Again, Believe Again; The Last
Addiction;* and *Mom, Sex Is No Big Deal!*

"*Surfing for God* is a profoundly necessary book for men. Not only does Cusick connect our sexual struggles and desires to our spirituality, he demonstrates through his own redemptive journey how to embrace the brokenness we carry, and live out of that place. This is where a true and centered life is found. I'm thrilled that this book is available for those haunted by sexual struggle, and have found it deeply encouraging in my own story."

—CHARLIE LOWELL
Jars of Clay

"Michael gets at the heart of a critical issue in the Body of Christ, one of which we tend to see only the tip of the iceberg. I deeply appreciate many of his keen insights, observations, and practical helps. My hope is that many will be set free to fully enjoy the grace of the gospel."

—DOUG NUENKE
U.S. President, The Navigators

"With great clarity and skill Michael John Cusick exposes the most rampant sin pathology of our time. Then with precision, he reveals how to excise it to restore spiritual and relational health. Whether you, a friend, or a loved one is suffering this malady, you will find *Surfing for God* your lifesaving manual for soul surgery."

—DAVID STEVENS
M.D., CEO, Christian Medical & Dental Association

"*Surfing for God* is a breakthrough work for men that goes beyond accountability groups and explores the roots of our inordinate passions and misplaced hungers. Drawing from Scripture, brain research, contemplative spiritual practices, and years of working through his own brokenness, Michael has crafted a work of hope where death is exchanged for life, shame is exchanged for vitality and compulsion is exchanged for deep connection. This book should be a well-worn copy for men and those who work with men."

—DR. ERIC SWANSON
Leadership Network, Co-author of *The Externally
Focused Church* and *To Transform a City*

"All of us have addictions—some to success and approval, others to pornography and other vices. *Surfing for God* is a truly helpful resource for those struggling with painful and destructive addictions to pornography and sexual sin. The forthright-ness of the author—one who is on his own healing journey—will be a blessing and a guide for all who struggle to take the journey from this particular bondage to the freedom that comes in embracing that which is life indeed."

—RUTH HALEY BARTON
Founder, Transforming Center, Author of *Invitation to
Solitude and Silence* and *Sacred Rhythms*

"The last thing we need is another book on sex that peddles platitudes or hawks simplistic solutions. Michael does neither. Tending to both the feral and the tender places in the masculine soul, the words on these pages burrow in and do a deep work."

—WINN COLLIER
Author of *Holy Curiosity*

"I am convinced this remarkable book is the answer to the prayers of people desperate for hope and freedom. Cusick's genius lies in the way he masterfully weaves his clinical expertise with the story of his own recovery to point those in the grip of an epidemic affliction toward healing and restoration."

—IAN MORGAN CRON
Counselor, Author of *Chasing Francis* and *Jesus, My Father, the CIA, and Me*

"*Surfing for God* is a deeply thoughtful and comprehensive resource for any man who is serious about finding freedom from sexual sin. Indispensable for church and ministry leaders!"

—STEVE SILER
Executive Director, Music for the Soul,
Producer of *Somebody's Daughter: A Journey to Freedom from Pornography*

"This book is a breath of a fresh air for men who have been trying so hard to break free from the shackles of porn and yet continue to struggle. In a wonderfully authentic and life-giving way, Michael Cusick shows us that there is hope and it is found, not in trying harder, but in our embracing the truth and power of the gospel. I want every man in my church to read this book. It is that significant."

—ALAN KRAFT
Senior Pastor, Christ Community Church,
Author of *Good News for Those Trying Harder*

"Michael Cusick simply will not let men settle for petty attempts to resolve their war with sexual struggles. He challenges men to explore their hearts and discover a profound passion that can never be satisfied with the emptiness of pornography. He leads us through his personal journey and invites us to connect our deepest desires to the hope of all desire—God."

—MICHAEL MISJA, PH.D.
Co-founder, North Coast Family Foundation,
Co-author of *Thriving Despite a Difficult Marriage*

"This isn't just another book telling you not to look at porn; it's an invitation to freedom and renewal. With love and grace dripping from every word, Michael leads you on a journey to discover your deepest desires and truest identity as God's beloved child. This is far more than a simple change in behavior, this book is a doorway into a new way of living."

—MICHAEL HIDALGO
Lead Pastor, Denver Community Church

"Working with porn-addicted college students for over a decade, I've learned that porn is just a symptom of broken masculinity, the cure for which is not found in trying or praying harder, finding accountability, just saying 'no', or setting up safeguards. But there is a Cure. Michael Cusick flat out knows men, and in *Surfing for God* he offers truth, demands deep reflection, gives hope, cheers you on, and invites you on a journey to recover your God-given masculinity. No gimmicks here, just truth that will set you free."

—DR. RYAN T. HARTWIG
Assistant Professor of Communication, Azusa Pacific University

"Michael brings hope and help in this masterful book. I encourage every man and every parent to read it."

—BOB ROBERTS, JR.
Senior Pastor, NorthWood Church
Author of *Real-Time Connections*; *Globalization*; and *Transformation*

"*Surfing for God* is a practical, gutsy, honest, biblical answer from the trenches. It addresses, head on, one of the greatest crises sweeping the church today. I highly recommend it!"

—PETER SCAZZERO
Senior Pastor, New Life Fellowship Church,
Author of *Emotionally Healthy Church* and *Emotionally Healthy Spirituality*

# SURFING FOR GOD

Discovering The Divine Desire
Beneath Sexual Struggle

## MICHAEL JOHN CUSICK

**THOMAS NELSON**
*Since 1798*

NASHVILLE   DALLAS   MEXICO CITY   RIO DE JANEIRO

Published in Nashville, Tennessee, by Thomas Nelson. Thomas Nelson is a trademark of Thomas Nelson, Inc.

Author is represented by the literary agency of Dudley Delffs, Ph.D., Creative Fidelity, Inc.

Thomas Nelson, Inc., titles may be purchased in bulk for educational, business, fundraising, or sales promotional use. For information, please e-mail SpecialMarkets@ ThomasNelson.com.

Unless otherwise indicated, Scripture quotations are taken from the Holy Bible, New International Version®, NIV®. Copyright © 1973, 1978, 1984, 2011 by Biblica, Inc.™ Used by permission of Zondervan. All rights reserved worldwide. www.zondervan.com. Unless otherwise indicated, quotations are from the 1984 edition. Quotations marked UPDATED NIV are from the 2011 edition.

Scripture quotations marked ESV are from THE ENGLISH STANDARD VERSION. © 2001 by Crossway Bibles, a division of Good News Publishers.

Scripture quotations marked KJV are from the King James Version (public domain).

Scripture quotations marked MSG are from The Message by Eugene H. Peterson. © 1993, 1994, 1995, 1996, 2000. Used by permission of NavPress Publishing Group. All rights reserved.

Scripture quotations marked NASB are from the NEW AMERICAN STANDARD BIBLE®, © The Lockman Foundation 1960, 1962, 1963, 1968, 1971, 1972, 1973, 1975, 1977, 1995. Used by permission.

Scripture quotations marked NKJV are from THE NEW KING JAMES VERSION. © 1982 by Thomas Nelson, Inc. Used by permission. All rights reserved.

Scripture quotations marked NLT are taken from the Holy Bible, New Living Translation. © 1996. Used by permission of Tyndale House Publishers, Inc., Wheaton, Illinois 60189. All rights reserved.

In some instances, names, dates, locations, and other details have been purposely changed to protect the identities and privacy of those discussed in this book.

### Library of Congress Cataloging-in-Publication Data

Cusick, Michael John, 1964–
  Surfing for God : discovering the divine desire beneath sexual struggle / Michael John Cusick.
    p. cm.
  Includes bibliographical references (p.    ).
  ISBN 978-0-8499-4723-0 (trade paper)
  1. Pornography—Religious aspects—Christianity. 2. Christian men—Religious life. 3. Men—Psychology. 4. Sex—Religious aspects—Christianity. I. Title.
  BV4597.6.C87 2012
  241'.667—dc23
                                                           2011053192

*Printed in the United States of America*

HB 11.02.2017

To my beloved,

**Julianne,**

*whose kindness and courage*

*free me to fly.*

*And to my father,*

**James Edward Cusick,**

*whose life is*

*a living parable of redemption.*

# contents

The pursuit of purity is not about the suppression of lust, but about the reorientation of one's life to a larger goal.

—DIETRICH BONHOEFFER

introduction

# What's Better than Porn?

A rabbi and his young disciple sat side by side under the shade of a large oak tree.

"Help me, Rabbi," said the disciple. "I am a double-minded man. The law of the Lord tells me, 'The Lord is my Shepherd and I shall not be in want.' But oh, how I want!"

The rabbi's face revealed a trace of a smile, but he remained silent.

"And Rabbi," said the younger man, "the law of the Lord tells me that my soul finds rest in God alone. But oh, how my soul finds rest in everything else!"

The rabbi's face revealed the same trace of a smile, but still he remained silent.

"And Rabbi," said the student, "the man after God's own heart told us to ask and seek after only one thing—to gaze upon the beauty of the Lord and seek Him in His temple. But my heart seeks after so many things." The student lowered his voice to a whisper. "And the beauty I secretly gaze upon brings me shame. How will I ever become a man after God's own heart when I am so unfaithful?"

With this the rabbi let go of all constraint and began to laugh, his eyes sparkling. "My son," said the rabbi. "Listen to the story I am about to tell you.

"Long ago, a skylark flew above the parched and desolate ground of the desert. Times were hard for all living things, and worms were not easy to come by for a creature of the air. Even so, the skylark sang a winsome song day after day as he sought his daily portion. As each day passed, the difficulty of finding food grew more extreme. In his hunger he began to grow restless. And in his restlessness he forgot how to sing."

The rabbi paused for a moment, wiped his brow, and exhaled deeply. The student sat attentively on the edge of his seat but wondered what this story had to do with becoming a man after God's own heart.

In a whisper the rabbi continued. "One day the skylark heard an unfamiliar voice. It was the voice of a traveling peddler, and the skylark could not believe what the peddler seemed to be selling. 'Worms! Worms! Mouthwatering worms!' cried the peddler. 'Come right up and get your delicious worms today!' Incredulous at this sudden good fortune, the skylark hopped closer to the peddler, drawing nearer to this manna from heaven.

"'Worms today! Two worms for one feather!' said the peddler. At the mention of worms, the skylark felt a pang of hunger, and suddenly he understood. *My feathers are many*, thought the skylark, imagining the taste of the worms in his beak. *Surely I will not miss just two small feathers.* So, unable to resist any longer, the skylark plucked two of his smallest feathers and surrendered them to the peddler, who, unbeknownst to the skylark, was the unholy one in disguise.

"As promised, the skylark had his choice of the fattest, juiciest worms he had ever seen. And all without needing to dig and claw in the unyielding ground! So the skylark took hold of four glistening worms and swallowed them. *Such small sacrifice, yet such great reward*, the skylark told himself. *Two small feathers is of no concern to me.* With his stomach full, the skylark stepped from his high perch and began to soar. And as he did, he began to sing once again.

"The next day the skylark swooped and sang until he met the nefarious peddler once again. Just as before, the peddler offered two worms for one feather. So the skylark feasted on the luscious worms until he had his fill. And so it went day after day. Times were still hard for all living things, and worms were still not easy to come by for creatures of the air.

"One day, after finishing the worms, the skylark attempted to take flight. Instead of soaring, he plummeted to the ground with a thud. Stunned but grateful to be alive, the skylark realized he had no more feathers. Of course, he could no longer fly."

The rabbi paused for so long that the disciple thought the story was over. He responded to his teacher by saying he would ponder the meaning of the story.

"Ah, but the story continues," said the rabbi. Sitting down, he exhaled deeply again. "Once the skylark realized he had given up his feathers and could not fly, he came to his senses," said the rabbi. "Desperate, he hopped and stumbled through the desert, gathering worms. A small one here, a small one there. After several days of striving and toil, he had a small pile of worms and returned to the peddler. 'Here are enough worms to exchange for my feathers—I need them back.'

"The devil, however, just laughed and said, 'You can't get your feathers back! You got your worms, and I've got your feathers. And after all, a deal is a deal!' And with that, he disappeared into thin air."

As the rabbi finished speaking, the young apprentice noticed a tear running down his teacher's cheek. "Rabbi, why the tear?" the disciple asked.

"The heart of God breaks when we give away our feathers for worms," the rabbi answered. "But even more, His heart breaks when we try to buy our feathers back. For only God can restore our feathers."

After a long silence the disciple asked, "And Rabbi, why were you laughing before you told me the story?" The rabbi turned, his moist eyes now twinkling again. "I laughed with joy because I have seen your heart. In your heart there is a song. And with your heart you will learn to fly."[1]

**xxx**

You and I were created to fly. But something has gone terribly wrong. Our ancient predecessors Adam and Eve were deceived by a serpent and forfeited paradise with God. The skylark was deceived by a traveling peddler and lost his ability to fly. Adam and Eve lost their innocence and covered themselves with fig leaves. The skylark lost its feathers and tried to buy them back. In my line of work, barely a day goes by that I don't hear a story about a man losing his feathers in exchange for pornography.

And though the feathers are not literal, the losses are devastating. Men are losing trust, reputation, and self-respect. They are losing marriages or other relationships. They are losing jobs, ministries, and careers. They are losing strength, purpose, and freedom. And they are losing the external self and the public identity that they work so hard to establish and maintain. After crash-landing from their own internal implosions, they are left lying on the ground.

Of course, when we experience such loss, it also affects wives, children, friends, congregations, and communities. Everyone loses when it comes to porn. It's tempting to think that there's nothing wrong with a porn habit, that no one gets hurt. We think we're protecting our wives by not telling them. We think we're providing ourselves with a few minutes of vacation from the variety of stressors in our days. No matter how we may justify or rationalize it, in two decades of counseling, not one man has told me that pornography made him a better man, husband, father, employee, minister, or friend.

Amid their stories of loss, I regularly hear men say two things. First, "I am tired of how little porn delivers." Despite our God-given attraction to the female form and our proclivity for visual stimulation, porn leaves us empty. We are tired of the using, the deception, the hiddenness, and the damage to our souls. Mostly we are tired of compulsively seeking something that promises so much but delivers so little. It's like waking up on Christmas morning day after day, eager to open the gift we've dreamed of all year, but discovering an empty box beneath the colorful wrapping paper and bow.

The second comment I hear men make is, "I am tired of the never-ending battle over lust." A battle that so often leads to defeat. Borrowing from the shampoo bottle instructions, I call it the "lather, rinse, repeat" cycle. First, it begins with getting clean—genuine remorse and sincere repentance. Promising God that we won't go there again. Then, for reasons we don't really understand, we go there again. Eventually, when our shame overwhelms us, or perhaps we've been discovered, we come clean again. But this time we tell somebody and find an accountability partner. Finally, we commit to a new strategy by redoubling our efforts, trying even harder, checking in more often with our accountability partner, and maybe reading our Bibles more. It's lather, rinse, repeat—with the emphasis on repeat. And the saddest part of this cycle is that most men see no alternative. We're seemingly stuck with two choices: either suppress our passions or give in and indulge them. We know in our hearts that porn is not God's best for our lives. But in the heat of the moment, it seems as if there's nothing better than porn. *We desperately need another way to live.*

The gospel—the life-giving good news of Jesus Christ—presents us with another way. But why do we fail to see the connection between our struggles with pornography and Jesus' promise of free-dom? We *believe* that the gospel can set us free, but we don't have a clue how this happens. We *believe* we can do all things through Christ who strengthens us, but too often this amounts to Jesus helping us flex our moral muscles as we tag-team wrestle the problem to the ground. For most men seeking to follow Jesus, connecting the power of God's grace to their struggle with lust and pornography remains a mystery.

If you are reading this book, you are probably battling against porn, trying to avoid porn, or you care about someone who is in the battle. If you are losing the battle, please read closely: *following Jesus consists of so much more than trying harder and white-knuckling your way through it.* You can be free. God has charted a path to freedom that men before you have walked. You can discover this path leading to authentic transformation in your soul, a path that consists of so much more than sin management. You also need to know that your masculine soul is deeper and truer than your desire for porn. Part of you longs to walk intimately with God. You want to be like David, the man after God's own heart, who wrote, "I run in the path of your commands, for you have set my heart free" (Ps. 119:32).

If you are trying to avoid getting caught in the snare of porn, I have good news for you too. You can walk in the way of wisdom, so that your heart feels passionate and alive. And if you care about someone who is in the battle or trying to avoid it, through this book you will find knowledge and understanding to help you identify the real issues contributing to sexual struggles so you can offer grace, hope, and guidance.

In the first part of this book, you will discover why struggles with porn are really not about sex. You will also identify the mistaken reasons men give for why they struggle with porn. And you will understand what porn offers on a level beneath what is skindeep. Finally, you will learn the seven God-given desires that lie below men's struggle with porn.

In the next section you will learn why breaking free from porn is so difficult. You will also discover why our brokenness is essential in the journey from lust to love. Then, in the discussion about the spiritual roots of addiction, you will look at the ways we avoid and control pain and how this relates to using pornography. And you will explore the nature of shame and how you can overcome it. Last, I will discuss the common cycle of how men become ensnared with porn.

The third part gets to the fun stuff. In this section you will unearth a lost treasure of the gospel. By discovering the reality of your new heart in Christ, you will understand that God has given us desires that go deeper than any desire for porn. You will recognize the need to fight against darkness as a spiritual warrior. And you will establish a clear understanding of how porn subverts your brain and capacity for intimacy.

The last section brings it all together. You will read about the specific path to freedom and wholeness. This includes learning about the life of Christ within you and how this is nurtured through solitude and attentiveness. You will learn about how to care for your soul and meet deep God-given needs in healthy ways. And finally, you will understand God's patterns for bringing about change.

Many approaches exist for healing compulsive sexual behaviors like porn addiction. By offering my framework, I am not in any way criticizing other approaches. From twelve-step groups to inner healing programs, from accountability partners to men's groups seeking sexual integrity, God uses a variety of resources to bring healing. My purpose here is to describe in biblical and spiritual terms a path to walk that may supplement any of these other approaches or stand on its own.

The problem with pornography is real. But God's eagerness to work in our hearts and bring healing is central to what we believe as followers of Jesus. One of the main reasons the gospel is good news is that God has a unique way of taking the very struggles that have become barriers to knowing Him more intimately—like struggles with pornography—and turning them into bridges. Are you ready to take this barrier of porn and let it become a bridge to life?

1

# Getting Your Feathers Back

*Sometimes God brings gifts into our lives that make our
hands bleed when we open the package. But inside
we discover what we've been looking for all our lives.*

—SHEILA WALSH

FBI Raids Escort Service.

Shivers raced down my spine as I inhaled deeply. I never expected to see this headline on the front page of the *Cleveland Plain Dealer*. A major sting operation on a local prostitution service made big-time news because several well-known professional athletes were involved. The FBI had confiscated the owner's little black book, complete with names and intimate details of customers. My name was hiding in that little black book.

Instantly my worst fears came true. At only twenty-four years old, my secret immoral life, which I had worked so hard to conceal, was about to be exposed: My porn addiction and frequent trips to adult bookstore video booths. My promiscuity, including the club hopping that none of my friends or ministry colleagues had any idea about. The alcohol abuse that became increasingly necessary to numb my shame, depression, and self-hatred. The massage parlors. The strip clubs. The endless cruising for sex-for-pay on darkened streets. And finally, the escort services—an innocent sounding euphemism for high-priced prostitution services that I couldn't afford but also couldn't stop myself from using.

In utter panic, my imagination launched into overdrive. I thought about the legal fallout. I imagined my mug shot in the paper. I pictured myself in handcuffs and an orange jumpsuit, standing before a judge. I envisioned myself locked behind bars, cornered by a gang of angry, tattooed cell mates. Then I imagined my friends and family and all the questions they would shoot at me. Who is this Michael we never knew? How could you do such disgusting things? What kind of person are you, anyway? All these questions I asked myself as I projected my shame and anxiety onto those I loved.

Somehow, I mindlessly endured that calamitous day, although I knew that the burning nausea in my gut would never go away. I felt utterly isolated. I couldn't trust anyone with my story. But with the likelihood of this news going public, I knew I had to talk to someone. That evening I phoned my sister and asked her to meet me. Sitting in her car in an empty parking lot, I poured out my story as the tears flowed and my face burned with shame. After offering immense grace and kindness, she gave me the number of a Christian counselor. The next morning I phoned and made an appointment.

Fast-forward twenty-four hours. I waited in the counselor's lobby. Right at the top of the hour, the door to the waiting room opened and out stepped Mike. As I sized him up, I realized he didn't fit my expectations for a counselor. For one thing, he was tall and masculine—not like the mild-mannered, neurotic-looking TV shrinks. He motioned me into the inner sanctum of his office, where I nervously made a wisecrack about lying on the couch, Freudian-style. I expected at least a chuckle, or some kind of reaction, but Mike just sat in his chair, unaffected.

"How can I be of help?" he asked, wasting no time and looking right into me.

*This guy doesn't mess around,* I thought. *A little chitchat would be nice before I spill the beans.* But I wasn't there to mess around, either. So I took the plunge and told him things I had never told another human being. Over forty-five minutes I talked nonstop with an air of bravado and repartee that I had long ago mastered for situations such as this. With a smile on my face and in my best storytelling persona, I told him about the sexual abuse that occurred throughout my childhood. He learned about my early exposure to pornography and my addiction to porn magazines, videos, adult video arcades, and massage parlors. I confessed to him my history with prostitutes and escort services. Through all of this he just listened as if none of this shocked him.

I spoke as if Mike and I were old friends just having a beer together, cracking jokes and telling stories I thought would make him laugh. But I couldn't elicit any kind of response apart from his strong, kind, unwavering presence. After listening for nearly an hour, Mike conspicuously lifted his arm, looked at his watch, and spoke his first words since asking how he could help.

"We're almost out of time. I'd like to offer a few thoughts."

*It's about time,* I thought. It's pretty unnerving to talk for fifty minutes about stuff you've never told anyone without hearing any response. I listened for his verdict.

"I have a comment and a question," he began. "First, the comment. *You strike me as a very lonely man.*"

Eight simple words. But they knocked the emotional wind out of me. My body language and facial expression didn't change, but a swirl of unpleasant emotions rose inside of me. I wasn't sure why, but I wanted to get out of that room. Then Mike continued.

"And now my question," he said with complete gentleness. "*Are you ever at a loss for words?*"

If his comment knocked the wind out of me, his question wrapped its hands around my windpipe. Suddenly I couldn't breathe.

*Isn't that totally socially inappropriate?* I thought reflexively. But deep down I knew he'd nailed me. After less than one hour together, this stranger uttered two sentences that exposed my bruised and stubborn heart. With uncanny accuracy he summed up something about me that I knew was true but couldn't admit. Hiding beneath the veneer of a finely crafted Christian image was a profoundly lonely boy-man. I was as uncomfortable in my own skin as any poser who ever existed. I was a broken man.

My life proved author Gerald May's assertion that self-deception is one of the chief characteristics of addiction.[1] You may find it strange to know that in all the years of my struggle with sexual sin, I never saw myself as a broken man. But brokenness was the very thing I couldn't acknowledge and tried to avoid by relentlessly working harder and harder to conceal the cracks in my soul.

In fact, shortly after becoming a Christian, I wrote a phrase attributed to Charles Spurgeon on the inside cover of my Bible: "A Bible that's falling apart is usually owned by someone who isn't." Right there, in large print and all caps, I established the cardinal rule for my fledgling faith. No falling apart. No weakness. Hold it together whatever the cost. Spurgeon's message was clear to my mind. A broken life—a life that's falling apart—and a life of intimacy with Christ were incompatible. So I set out to read my Bible until it was dog-eared and falling apart with the hidden hope that my very broken life would hold together. But then I lost my feathers and discovered I could no longer fly.

I will never forget the first time I made a serious effort to get my feathers back so I could fly again. One day in my junior year of high school—with utter sincerity and a genuine desire to honor God—I made a decision: porn and compulsive masturbation would no longer be a part of my life. As a brand-new follower of Jesus, I made the decision to clean house. When no one else was home, I grabbed my stack of hard-core porn magazines from under my mattress and carried them down to the basement incinerator where we burned our garbage.

With a strange mixture of anxiety and pride, I opened the incinerator, placed the magazines inside, and said good-bye to my struggles with lust, masturbation, and pornography. I lit a match and held it to a centerfold that burned with the fiery intensity it used to ignite in me. As I closed the lid, I imagined my compulsive sin going up in smoke with the paper those illicit images were printed on. A little while later I checked to make sure they had completely burned, not wanting anyone to discover my shameful secret. All that remained was a pile of gray ash. Feelings of relief and hope rose inside me in a way I had never experienced. This was the end.

You can probably guess what happened next. Months later I repeated the same pattern, except with a new stash of porn. I hoped to get my feathers back. Instead I discovered once again that I couldn't fly.

## ALL OF US SHARE A BIPOLAR STRUGGLE

In listening to thousands of men—friends, acquaintances, students, clients—I have heard a thousand variations of sending our struggles up in smoke, only to discover that after the smoke has risen, the struggle still lies hidden in the ashes. In the old PC (pre-computer) days, men tried throwing away videotapes or burning magazines. Today they delete their porn-saturated hard drives or shred their hidden stash of DVDs. Their efforts come from deep and meaningful commitments of genuine surrender—only to return to masturbation and porn. Then follows the onset of increased shame, self-contempt, distance from God, loss of confidence, loss of intimacy, and loss of passion. Finally, they give up.

Their passions swing like a pendulum. First they swing toward the familiar pattern of lust that leads to sexual sin. The power of erotic beauty becomes so irresistible that they risk anything and everything for its pursuit. Then they swing toward a genuine desire to walk with God and follow His ways, to be better husbands and fathers, men worthy of respect. Back and forth it goes.

Scripture addresses this bipolar struggle with stunning clarity. The apostle Paul gave us an honest description of our battle with sin. Though he wasn't directly referring to sexual sin, his description of the pain, shame, confusion, and powerlessness resonates universally:

> What I don't understand about myself is that I decide one way, but then I act another, doing things I absolutely despise. So if I can't be trusted to figure out what is best for myself and then do it, it becomes obvious that God's command is necessary.
>
> But I need something more! For if I know the law but still can't keep it, and if the power of sin within me keeps sabotaging my best intentions, I obviously need help! I realize that I don't have what it takes. I can will it, but I can't do it. I decide to do good, but I don't really do it; I decide not to do bad, but then I do it anyway. My decisions, such as they are, don't result in actions. Something has gone wrong deep within me and gets the better of me every time.
>
> It happens so regularly that it's predictable. The moment I decide to do good, sin is there to trip me up. I truly delight in God's commands, but it's pretty obvious that not all of me joins in that delight. Parts of me covertly rebel, and just when I least expect it, they take charge.
>
> I've tried everything and nothing helps. I'm at the end of my rope. Is there no one who can do anything for me? Isn't that the real question? (Rom. 7:15–24 MSG)

Paul may as well have been reading our e-mail. Actually, by drawing from his own struggles, he brilliantly captured the inner workings of the human soul: the battle between flesh and spirit, the old man and the new man, right and wrong, and the difference between what we long for and what we settle for. The struggle was not unique to Paul; nor is it unique to anyone struggling with pornography and sexual sin. But Paul's authentic and vulnerable confession assures us that such a struggle doesn't automatically mean we're unbelievers or spiritually immature. The intensity of our struggle, which feels overwhelming, does not invalidate our faith.

In fact, identifying this struggle and acknowledging our failure to manage it gives us the hopeful building blocks of a growing belief and true maturity. Of course, we can remain stuck in this place Paul described. But no one wants to stay tied to the bungee cord of acting out and trying harder to do better—we end up with emotional whiplash. No, according to Paul, we are created for more than this snap-back-and-forth cycle. And he was only describing three-quarters of the message in the passage I just gave you. His critical point offers the heart of the good news: we can be free "through Jesus Christ our Lord" (v. 25).

## YOU WERE DESIGNED FOR MORE

Have you ever wondered what makes a certain act sinful and another not sinful? Why is it wrong to lie? Or kill? Or commit adultery? Who says viewing porn is wrong when our culture tries to reassure us that it's natural and normal—in fact, based on popular consumption and the ten-billion-dollar industry it generates, you're abnormal if you don't view porn!

One way of thinking about why something is sinful is to respond, "It says in the Bible that it's wrong." While true, God put dos and don'ts into the Bible because they reveal something much deeper about us. When God tells us not to commit adultery, He is telling us that doing this goes against our design. "Do not commit adultery" is

God's version of "Do not brush your teeth with a toaster" or "Do not grill steaks on a block of ice." It just can't accomplish what it was designed to do. Like sailing the seven seas in a Chevy pickup—it doesn't get the job done, and you put yourself at great risk.

Or consider porn this way. Wouldn't it be rather odd if a trained fighter pilot never left the hangar for fear of not knowing how to fly the jet? Or consider a gifted sculptor who never picked up his hammer and chisel because he couldn't find the perfect block of marble. What if a major-league baseball player didn't show up for practice because he spent all his time playing baseball on his Xbox? Or a master shipbuilder never sailed the open waters because his fantasy of the perfect seaworthy vessel kept him on dry ground?

This is what porn is like. It allures us with the image or fantasy of being with a woman, while preventing us from being able to actually engage with a *real* woman. Porn keeps us from flying the jet, getting in the game, or sailing the high seas. All because we settle for something that doesn't exist and will never satisfy us.

So how does porn go against our design as men and sabotage God's dream for us to live out our true identities? C. S. Lewis spoke to the heart of this question when he wrote about the soul damage caused by sexual fantasy (whether through masturbation or pornography) and what he called "imaginary women." Lewis described these imaginary women this way: "Always accessible, always subservient, calls for no sacrifices or adjustments, and can be endowed with erotic and psychological attractions which no real woman can rival. Among those shadow brides he is always adored, always the perfect lover; no demand is made on his unselfishness, no mortification ever imposed on his vanity."[2]

Lewis began with the assumption that sex is good, not bad—a gift to be enjoyed within God-designed boundaries. He also framed his words against the backdrop that "the main work of life is to come up and out of ourselves." Lewis assumed that God designed us to mature and become less focused on ourselves and more focused on loving others. When we fixate on porn, we choose to remain selfishly anchored to our own pleasure above all else. When we preoccupy ourselves with meeting our own needs and ignoring the needs of others—in this case, our wives, flesh-and-blood women, and not some Photoshopped model—then we stifle our spiritual growth. Lewis summed up the problem with pornography this way: "In the end, [imaginary women] become the medium through which he increasingly adores himself. After all, the main work of life is to come out of ourselves, out of the little, dark prison we are all born in. . . . All things are to be avoided which retard this process. The danger is that of coming to love the prison."[3]

Lewis calls us to remember what a man is made for: our deepest longing is to know God in the center of our being, and out of that place to offer ourselves for the sake of others. Augustine[4] taught about the theological idea of *incurvatus se*—a life turned in on itself. Porn successfully accomplishes this—it causes our soul to turn in on itself in self-absorbed isolation and shame. It diminishes our souls. It seduces a man to use women to meet a need in himself—without meeting any of her needs. And this act of "using" comes not only at her expense but also at the devastating cost of his own heart. We don't realize the price we pay until we feel empty and bankrupt inside.

You were created for something bigger than yourself. You were created for *excurvatus se*—a life lived outward. Not outward as in codependent or being a martyr. Not dying to self in a way where legitimate needs are neglected. But a life that flows from a deep source. A life that bears fruit. A life lived outwardly enhances, builds up, and causes the heart to flourish. Donald Miller has suggested that we are trees in the story of a forest. And that story of the forest is better than the story of the trees.[5] Pornography perverts and upends this idea with titillating images that invite us to live as if the story of the trees were the only story, and the story of the forest doesn't exist.

The purpose of this book is to go beyond the common "Just don't do it" strategy of sin management. Together, we will explore the truth of how you were meant to live and how you can get there so you can enjoy a new and better life in the forest. I invite you to stop looking at pictures of F-18s in combat and ships on the high seas, or playing baseball on your Xbox instead of eating the dust of a real baseball diamond. We'll do much more than that. You'll discover the thrill of getting into the game, flying the F-18, and sailing the ship so that pornography and lust lose their grip on your soul.

Please read closely: the deepest truth about you is that you *are* the F-18 pilot, created for combat. God designed you to be a hero— to focus your strength and courage on behalf of something and someone bigger than yourself. You *are* the major-league ballplayer, created with the offensive and defensive abilities to get in the game with a team of others on a common mission. God uniquely fashioned you to win games. To hit home runs. To steal bases. God chose you to play on His team.

## DISCOVERING A DEEPER DESIRE

On a cold winter night in 1994, my addiction to porn and illicit sex still held me firmly in its grip. That night, obsessed with my next fix, I began my typical ritual of acting out sexually. I sat in a familiar parking lot of a XXX bookstore, troubled by the routine I was about to perform even though I had carried it out too many times to count. I had a beautiful wife at home, but she was the last thing on my mind.

Less than a block from the porn store sat the Cathedral of the Immaculate Conception, a spectacular edifice that hosted Pope John Paul II earlier that year. Without warning, an impulse to set foot in that house of worship overwhelmed me. I walked toward the cathedral, hiked the tall steps, and opened the monolithic oak door. The cathedral was empty except for a custodian mopping the floor near the altar.

In the cathedral I sat in the back row of pews. The space and silence were terrifying. I couldn't remember the last time I had been alone and given any thought to the world within me. After a few minutes of struggling to pray, I stood and walked to the back corner, where dozens of votive candles were perched on a table. Mustering what little faith I had, I struck a match and lit a candle. I felt no magic and certainly no expectation that my simple action would make my struggles suddenly disappear. But I reconnected with something I had lost—my better self, my true self. As I raised the flame toward its mark, I voiced a prayer that came straight from my true heart: "God, I want more. I want more. I want more."

Then I returned to the pew and scribbled some thoughts in my journal. The building at that moment represented a metaphor for my soul—something empty, dimly lit, disconnected from others. At the same time the structure was glorious. Its buttresses and stained-glass windows pointed upward to something bigger, something beyond. Maybe I was like this cathedral—broken *and* glorious all at the same time. Maybe it wasn't too late for me to hope.

**2**

# It's Not About Sex

It's not the shouting of pornography that gives it so
much power over men. It is the whispering of the lie.

**—WILLIAM STRUTHERS,** *WIRED FOR INTIMACY*

Standing on the edge of the abyss, Frodo prepares to complete his
mission to save Middle-earth. After risking life and limb and battling
inconceivable odds, one task remains: to destroy the notorious gold
Ring by throwing it into the fires of Mordor. Obliterating the Ring
will break its power and set Middle-earth free from the grasp of darkness. No problem, right?

This scene appears in J. R. R. Tolkien's *The Return of the King*,
the final installment of his trilogy *The Lord of the Rings*. Whether
you've read the books or watched the movie series, you know that
the Ring is no ordinary piece of jewelry. It contains compelling
forces; those who behold it are at once captivated. Many have killed
or been killed in their attempts to possess its dark power.

So Frodo—an unlikely little Hobbit—finds himself entrusted
with destroying the Ring. Standing above the liquid flames, Frodo
experiences something altogether unexpected. Despite every good
intention, after he had fought the good fight, the Ring now capti-
vates *him*. In the heat of the moment, its seductive power entrances
him and he refuses to throw it in the fire. Frodo knows what he

*ought* to do and why he *should* do it. He understands that the fulfillment of his mission—and countless lives—hangs in the balance. But he just can't drop the Ring.

Meanwhile Sam, his best friend and faithful companion on the journey, witnesses the struggle. Standing back in disbelief, Sam shouts at the top of his lungs to throw the Ring into the fire. But Frodo can't let go. The force that motivated his mission now holds him captive.

You and I are caught in the same struggle as Frodo, but the power of porn is far from mythic. Like Frodo, we've been given a critical mission of epic proportions and eternal significance. We're charged with loving God and loving others so that the kingdom of God will become more real in our hearts and the world around us (Matt. 22:37–40). Deep in our hearts we want to fulfill the mission and kick back the powers of darkness. But we find ourselves giving in to something "less than," a counterfeit—porn.

## WHY CAN'T YOU JUST DROP THE RING?

Hardly anyone wakes up one morning and decides that he wants to cross his own boundaries, violate his values, and deceive himself and everyone around him. But for so many of us, that's exactly what happens. It happened to me. So let me ask *you* a question. If you share this struggle, why can't *you* throw the ring of pornography in the fire? And if, like me, you've thrown it in the fire, melting it in the flames, why does it keep rising, phoenixlike, from the ashes?

Right now, whether you know it or not, some deep-seated belief explains your preoccupation with lust and attraction to porn. Why does porn exert such great power over you? Why do you indulge? Maybe you attribute your compulsions to a sex drive that's in high gear. *If I weren't so horny all the time, I wouldn't struggle this way. But hey, I can't change my sexual urges.* Maybe you attribute your struggle to your partner's lack of desire or interest in sexual intimacy. *If my wife were more turned on or did what turns me on, if she'd just cut loose and be more uninhibited, then I wouldn't need porn.* Maybe you believe that your struggle with porn comes from your wife's appearance or lack of sex appeal in your eyes. *If my wife lost weight or got a boob job or dressed sexier, I'd be more interested in her.* Maybe you attribute your struggle to a lack of willpower. *If I could be more disciplined and focused, I know I could get over this. If I really tried harder, I could give up porn.*

Or maybe you've concluded that if you were a more spiritual person, then porn wouldn't be a problem. *If I read my Bible more, prayed more, and focused on God more, then He would help me avoid this temptation.* Or maybe you frame your struggle as a lack of accountability. *If I knew more people I could trust, guys who really understand what it's like, men I could come clean with, then I know I could control this.*

Whatever you believe is the cause, my prayer is that by the end of this book you will realize that your struggles with lust and porn are not actually about sex. I hope you will realize that the compulsion toward porn far exceeds the thrill of orgasm or appreciation for a woman's body proportions. It involves far more than viewing a new stimulating sexual position or a hotter, more provocative partner. In the same way, overeating is not about food—something else compels the food addict to eat an entire one-pound bag of M&M's in one sitting. Compulsive shopping is about so much more than needing more stuff to put in our garages or closets. So, too, our sexual lusts and preoccupations with porn point to more than naked bodies or illicit sex.

## SO WHAT *IS* IT ABOUT?

Two thousand years ago, a pastor named Paul offered guidance to a sexually broken and confused church under his care in the

Mediterranean city of Corinth: "There's more to sex than mere skin on skin. Sex is as much spiritual mystery as physical fact" (1 Cor. 6:16 MSG). Paul was explaining to these men and women who were involved in adultery, prostitution, and virtually every other kind of sexual sin, "What you're doing is not actually about sex." Beyond the obvious—bodies seeking and experiencing pleasure—all of us reach toward something we cannot see, touch, or comprehend on the physical level.

This truth is utterly profound. Understanding it helps us gain insight into why our sexuality can be so compulsive. If we seek on the physical level what can only be obtained on a spiritual level, then we set ourselves up for a never-ending cycle that only leads to desperation, despair, and bondage.

So if sex is as much spiritual mystery as physical pleasure, then what does that tell us? Almost a century ago, G. K. Chesterton wrote that the man who knocks on the brothel door is knocking for God. If he were writing today, he might say that the man who surfs the web for porn is surfing for God. If nothing else, this truth means that sex is a signpost to God. It also points us to the way He designed us as sexual beings—when we are most aligned with this design and intention, we are most powerful, complete, and fulfilled.

Maybe you've heard the saying that in a marriage the sexual relationship is a barometer for the relationship in general. When a husband and wife enjoy a healthy emotional, relational, and spiritual connection, most of the time good sex follows. In the same way, a man's sexual appetite is a barometer for what's going on inside his heart. Your sex drive consists of more than testosterone and the buildup of seminal fluid pressing for biological release, more than being visually stimulated and feeling aroused. Sexual arousal is an accumulation of your experiences, deep needs, and unconscious beliefs. Your heart shares a deep connection to your body parts. The way you are sexually aroused reflects what's happening deep in your soul, beyond your sexual organs. Indeed, sex is as much spiritual mystery as it is physical fact. The reality is that your heart needs something, and porn promises to meet that need.

## THE BROKEN PROMISES OF PORN

Frodo didn't shout, "The Ring is mine!" because he had a special affinity for jewelry. The Ring promised him something—infinite power and ultimate control. Like all idols, porn promises us something we desire. In reality, it overpromises and underdelivers.

To understand this more fully, let's revisit sin's original slick sales pitch to human hearts. In the garden of Eden, we clearly see that Adam and Eve didn't disobey God because they woke up one morning on the wrong side of the bed. Nor did they eat the forbidden fruit because they weren't holding each other accountable. Something deeper and more compelling was going on that made the fruit virtually irresistible.

> The serpent told the Woman, "You won't die. God knows that the moment you eat from that tree, you'll see what's really going on. You'll be just like God, knowing everything, ranging all the way from good to evil."
> When the Woman saw that the tree looked like good eating and realized what she would get out of it—she'd know everything!—she took and ate the fruit and then gave some to her husband, and he ate. (Gen. 3:4–6 MSG)

Eve didn't just take the fruit and give some to her husband because she was especially weak that day or because she didn't have her quiet time that morning. The serpent suggested that God was not telling the truth, and as a result it seems that Eve began questioning whether God was really who He said He was. After all, the serpent implied, if God told her something that wasn't true ("You will die"), how could she trust God about not eating the fruit?

Oswald Chambers claimed that all sin is rooted in the suspicion that God is not really good.[1] Eve ate the fruit because she believed she would get a payoff. On a physical level it tasted good, but it also promised some kind of satisfaction to her soul. Her heart hungered for life, and after the serpent suggested that God might not really be all that trustworthy, she chose life—apart from God. Sin always promises something, and porn constantly promises to meet our deepest longings as men and women—without a cost. From my experiences, research, and observations, porn promises fulfillment of five key desires, all without responsibility.

## PORN PROMISES VALIDATION OF OUR MANHOOD WITHOUT REQUIRING STRENGTH

When talking with men about their struggles with porn, I often ask what seems like a random question. *Where in your life do you typically feel the strongest and manliest?* Most of the time this stumps them because they don't have a category in their minds for thinking about their strength and masculinity. But then, almost to a man, they relate to feeling strong at work, playing sports, doing ministry, or engaging in some other hobby. *In more than twenty years of counseling, however, I've never heard a man initially respond by saying that he felt the manliest and strongest in relation to his wife, fiancée, or girlfriend.* Most men don't feel terribly strong or adequate in the presence of a real, live woman—whether they're the CEO of a Fortune 500 company, a decorated war hero, or a seasoned pastor. And yet, God designed our masculine souls to be energized by offering ourselves on behalf of our female counterparts.

Enter porn, which allows us to have our cake ("I feel strong and masculine") and eat it too (no strength or masculinity required).

"What makes pornography so addictive," wrote John Eldredge, "is that more than anything else in a man's life, it makes him feel like a man without ever requiring a thing of him."[2] The allure of porn is that—contrary to a woman in real life—it makes us feel like men, and it never rolls its eyes at us or rolls over in bed. Porn never reminds us of our failures, flaws, or shortcomings. It doesn't evaluate our appearances or performances, our net worths or credentials. Porn doesn't tell us to clip our toenails or put the toilet seat down. Porn doesn't care if we are sullen, irritable, overweight, selfish—even undesirable. Porn's only requirement of a man is a pulse—and maybe the click of a mouse.

Struggles with porn confirm our suspicions that we do not have what it takes to be a man. Somewhere deep inside we believe that we lack the strength to relate to a real woman. As Robert Jensen wrote, porn beckons us with a promise: "What brings us back, over and over, is the voice in our ears, the soft voice that says, 'It's okay, you really are a man, you really can be a man, and if you come into my world, it will all be there, and it will all be easy.' . . . Pornography knows men's weakness. It speaks to that weakness, softly. . . . But for most men, it starts with the soft voice that speaks to our deepest fear: That we aren't man enough."[3]

So in the absence of felt strength, we turn to porn as if it were steroids for our soul. In our minds, porn makes us bigger, stronger, and more desirable. We get our fix and affirm our manhood. The seductive images reliably tell us that we are *the* man. But as we do with real steroids, we risk porn's damaging side effects and possible public disgrace. Without this drug, we become just another guy and wonder if we make the cut. C. S. Lewis understood this when he wrote that every time a man masturbates, he chips away at his manhood.

Porn gives us permission to avoid asking the hard questions about our masculine souls. *Why do I feel weak in the presence of a particular woman? Why is so much at stake when I relate to her? Why do I feel I have so little to offer?* But when we scrape together the courage to face these questions, we discover life-changing truths about ourselves that can set us free. Truths that will lead us to something better than porn.

## PORN PROMISES SEXUAL FULFILLMENT WITHOUT RELATIONSHIP

On the corner of a major intersection in Denver, a prominent billboard advertises an adult store selling porn DVDs. Its message is short and sweet: "Cheaper Than Dating!" It may seem funny or clever at first, but the message couldn't be any clearer: Are you looking for sexual satisfaction? Do you desire sexual pleasure? Don't even bother with a real woman. Just satisfy your appetite from our all-you-can-eat buffet of endless sexual variety. Satisfaction guaranteed with the click of your remote control.

The first time I saw this billboard, I didn't know whether to laugh or to cry, mostly because it hit so close to home. One of my claims to fame in high school was that I never went to a dance and never went on a date. No homecoming dance. No winter ball. No prom. Once, a girl I actually had a crush on asked me to a dance. I wanted to go with her, but I lied and told her I was busy.

I didn't turn her down because I wasn't attracted to girls or to her in particular—as I mentioned, I had a crush on her. I was simply too terrified to move toward a girl with any kind of passion. Unwilling to put my budding masculine strength on the line by pursuing any kind of romantic involvement, I played the role of the safe guy. One of the guys who could relate to girls as a friend, make them laugh, but never be expected to move toward them romantically. As long as I was the safe guy, I could have my cake and eat it too.

A few times in high school I got close to pursuing girls I liked. But just when my confidence reached a certain point, I would find myself inescapably drawn to porn. I would masturbate, and then I would ultimately lose any sense of confidence that I had anything to offer a woman. With my regular intake of soul steroids, I steadily chipped away at my manhood, convincing myself that I didn't need a girlfriend. Even though, deep inside, I desperately longed for one.

## PORN PROMISES INTIMACY WITHOUT REQUIRING RISK AND SUFFERING

I recently asked a man I was counseling to tell me how he felt about conflict. "You mean, like, conflict in the Middle East?" he said.

Not exactly. "How do you feel about conflict in your marriage and closest relationships?" I asked. Without hesitating he related that he wrote the words "avoid conflict" at the top of his to-do list every day. We both laughed. Then I asked, "Do you see the connection between your goal to avoid conflict and your addiction to porn and lust?"

At first he gave me a blank stare, as if I had just asked him if he could explain the connection between the invention of the internal combustion engine and the rise of capitalism. Then the lights started to come on. He began to realize that with his wife, family, coworkers, and friends, he never really exposed his heart. To avoid conflict he never shared what he really thought, felt, or wanted. As a young boy growing up in a family that prized heartless compliance and maintaining a rigid religious appearance, he learned to avoid disappointing others.

Living like this makes intimacy difficult, to say the least. In his marriage, rather than risk moving toward his wife and sharing his heart, he turned to porn to meet his need for intimacy. Porn allowed him to give his heart to something that could not directly hurt him or reject him. Behind his struggle for porn stood a self-protective commitment to keep his heart safe from the disappointment and rejection he had come to know so well.

C. S. Lewis described every man's struggle with vulnerability this way:

To love at all is to be vulnerable. Love anything, and your heart will be wrung and possibly broken. If you want to be sure of keeping your heart intact you must give your heart to no one, not even an animal. Wrap it carefully around with hobbies and little luxuries, avoid all entanglements. Lock it up safely in the casket of your selfishness. And in that casket, safe, dark, motionless, airless, it will not change, it will not be broken. It will become unbreakable, impenetrable and irredeemable. The only place outside of heaven where you can be perfectly safe from the dangers of love is hell.[4]

Though at first they seem like a slice of heaven, porn and lust are a kind of hell. They offer us false intimacy, safeguarding our hearts from the perils of true intimacy. But porn ultimately makes our hearts incapable of the very thing we long for. Our hearts become incapable of love.

## PORN PROMISES PASSION AND LIFE WITHOUT CONNECTION TO YOUR SOUL

In the film *American Beauty*, Lester Burnham is a forty-two-year-old office worker who is going through a midlife crisis and has lost his soul. At the beginning of the film, he narrates his life, divulging that he will be dead within one year. "In a way I'm dead already," he relates. "Look at me. Jerking off in the shower. This will be the high point of my day. It's all downhill from there."[5] Is this scene just an exploitive attempt at crude humor by some faithless Hollywood writer? I wish I could say this was the case. But for many men, porn *is* the high point of their days. It offers a reliable way to feel passion and life. Even if just for a moment.

Of course, as human beings created in God's image, we were designed to experience life. Jesus' words, "I came that they may have life and have it abundantly," highlight this truth (John 10:10 ESV).

We were meant to live life to the fullest. But for men who have lost their souls, the moments of escape, relief, or validation from porn become a substitute for the life Christ offers.

Awhile back my son and I spent the day snowmobiling at ten-thousand-feet elevation in Breckenridge, Colorado. Our time together was filled with high-speed, adrenaline-pumping adventure. At day's end I turned to my son, gave him a high five, and said, "Now, *this* is living!"

"This *is* living!" he replied.

Where in your life do you say, "*This* is living!"? If you don't have something in your life that regularly inspires adventure, risk, and passion, beware. Because if you don't, you will seek the counterfeit.

## PORN PROMISES POWER OVER WOMEN WITHOUT RESPONSIBILITY AND HUMILITY

Cliff had just completed his third sexual purity workshop when we first crossed paths. He was mystified as to why porn held him in its grip. But his marriage was in serious trouble, and he was highly motivated to get to the bottom of his addiction. While discussing his response to a recent marital conflict, I asked him if porn was a sneaky way of getting back at his wife. Cliff smiled sheepishly. His honesty was disarming.

"I know it's pretty immature," he said. "But it's my way of sticking it to my wife." He went on to describe a pattern that many men will recognize. When he and his wife argued, if she overspent, or if she declined his sexual advances, he turned to porn in order to make her pay.

"It's like when someone cuts me off in traffic," he explained to me. "They may be driving up ahead and not even know what they've done, but I'm flipping them the middle finger. That's what I've been doing with my wife." As our conversations continued, the focus shifted from porn to the deeper issue of why he felt so power-less with his wife. For Cliff, porn was only a symptom of a much deeper issue related to his broken masculinity.

Porn promises power over women another way. Images and scenes of women being humiliated, degraded, and violated for the pleasure of men are now commonplace online. What is this about? Most often, it speaks to the clinical issue of tolerance, the idea that more and more of the "drug" is required to get the same effect. When more of the drug can't bring about the desired effect, then it becomes necessary to change drugs. In the case of porn, changing drugs means seeking out scenes that are darker, edgier, and even more abusive. I've spoken with numerous men who began their online porn career by "innocently" searching for naked celebrity pics, but eventually ended up compulsively searching for violent and repulsive material they never could have imagined wanting before.

A man may feel legitimate power in the presence of a woman. But true power is never power *over* a woman. A man seeks power over a woman because he is empty, needy, and broken, and believes he must use her to fill himself. True power, the power that Jesus con-sistently demonstrated, is power *under*. True power never devalues, dehumanizes, coerces, or controls. Instead, it serves, gives sacrificially, and acts for the good of the other. Power under is the way of the cross, the way of humility. As men, we are called to live out our legitimate power with responsibility and humility.

## PORN PROMISES COMFORT AND CARE WITHOUT DEPENDING ON OTHERS

Raymond was a single seminary student who came to see me because he was tired of pretending. A charismatic and respected leader on campus, he would never be suspected of spending more than five hours every day involved in porn and cybersex. When we met, he wondered if he was even a Christian. Years of battling lust had left him defeated, and now he realized he needed serious help. To say he was covered in shame and self-loathing would be an understatement.

I listened to Raymond's story and learned that he grew up an only child, raised by a single mom. To make ends meet, she worked two jobs, leaving her with little time or energy for Raymond. By fourth grade, he had learned to wash his clothes and cook for himself. He spent several nights a week alone after school and regularly put himself to bed. Television became his main source of comfort. One night Raymond discovered that he could turn to the adult channels and listen to sexually explicit dialogue. Although the images were blocked out, the voices made him feel confused, excited, and comforted all at the same time. Soon he discovered masturbation, which he described as so powerful it was like "kissing the face of God." As he grew into his teenage years and beyond, he traded sexually explicit dialogue for online porn.

My first conversation with Raymond occurred more than ten years ago. Today he is free from sexual compulsion and serves as a minister and counselor to men struggling with their own sexual brokenness. The beginning of the end of his addiction started when he identified porn as the only way he could experience care and nurturing. It had never occurred to him that beneath his shame-filled compulsions were a hunger and thirst for something legitimate and good.

Have you ever asked yourself what's really going on beneath your craving for porn? What lies below your desire for a pleasurable, physical release? What is your heart's real desire, the legitimate need desperately crying out to be heard? Not only can you overcome your sexual struggles with porn, fantasy, and masturbation, but you can also enjoy life at a level you may have never experienced.

It's called *joy*.

## 3

# Insatiable Thirst

Lust is the craving for salt of a man who is dying of thirst.

**—FREDERICK BUECHNER**

Pulling out of the church parking lot, I cranked up the car radio as loud as it would go. I was trying to forget the worship service that had just hammered another nail into the coffin of my critically ill faith. The sermon started my downward spiral.

"If we can just align our desires with God's," the well-intentioned pastor had said, "then and only then will we win the battle over the sins and struggles that entangle us."

*Hmm. If only I could align my desires with God's,* I thought. That seemed like the story of my Christian life. After years of struggling with lust and porn, my life had escalated into a full-blown sexual addiction. So the idea of aligning my desires with God's seemed not only absurd but utterly exhausting.

The closing song was the shove that pushed me over the edge. As everyone around me joyfully praised God, I mouthed the words but couldn't utter a sound: ". . . and nothing I desire compares with You." Standing in the church sanctuary, I desperately wanted those words to be true, but I couldn't speak them. It had been far too long since those words *were* true for me. Honestly, God couldn't compare to most of what I desired—not the least of which was pornography and illicit sex. My cravings seemed too intense for even God to fill.

Discouraged and bored with my life, I drove to the nearest convenience store and bought a six-pack of beer with a credit card hovering near its limit. After driving aimlessly for an hour, I wandered into an area of Cleveland known for its easy access to sex and drugs. I had every intention of plunging into the abyss of my addiction despite my recent near miss with the newspaper article. But after cruising, trancelike, through those seedy streets, I suddenly realized that what I was about to do was utterly empty. I just didn't know what else to do. So I checked into a motel—alone, depressed, and desperate. Although I wasn't suicidal, I desperately wanted to escape my life. Nursing a warm beer, I masturbated and then fell asleep.

Several hours later, I awoke to the familiar wave of shame and sadness. This was a cycle I knew all too well. I got up, poured the rest of the beer down the sink, checked out of the motel, and drove home more lonely and hollow than I'd ever felt in my life. All the while I sensed that beneath my restless cravings, a thirst existed for something that all the sex and beer in the world could never satisfy. I just didn't know what it was or how to find it.

## ARE YOU THIRSTY?

*Aposia* is a medical term meaning "the absence of sensation of thirst."[1] The symptoms usually result from another condition or a disease. In and of itself, aposia is not life threatening. But for people unaware that they have it, the consequences of not taking in fluids—dehydration, electrolyte imbalance, and eventually cardiac arrest—can be deadly.

Over the years I have observed a spiritual counterpart to aposia: the loss of our sense or perception of *spiritual and relational* thirst.

Unlike the physical disease, which is relatively rare, the spiritual condition seems as widespread as the common cold. This shouldn't surprise us. After all, Scripture tells us that "hope deferred makes the heart sick" (Prov. 13:12). Who wants to live with hope, thirst, and longing if doing so could potentially make your heart sick?

Let's face it: hope is life giving, but to deeply and intensely desire something and not receive it can be virtually unbearable. On the other hand, the consequences of losing our sense of spiritual thirst can be just as dramatic as losing our physical thirst. How can we love God with all of our minds, hearts, souls, and strength when the desires of our hearts and souls are not operating at full capacity? Our souls' thirst is the core desire from which everything else in the Christian life flows.

Desire and thirst are central to Christianity. When Jesus of Nazareth invites people to follow Him, He first awakens desire. Jesus issues this invitation: "If anyone is thirsty, let him come to me and drink. Whoever believes in me, as the Scripture has said, streams of living water will flow from within him" (John 7:37–38).

Notice that Jesus placed a condition on His offer. The condition—"*if* anyone is thirsty"—tells us that we must recognize our thirst. This implies that some people listening to His offer of life simply won't recognize their deep longing. Some of the people listening to Jesus that day suffered from spiritual aposia.

So were the folks in Isaiah's time, because Jesus' words echo His heavenly Father's offer in the Old Testament: "Come, all you who are thirsty, come to the waters; and you who have no money, come, buy and eat! Come, buy wine and milk without money and without cost. Why spend money on what is not bread, and your labor on what does not satisfy?" (Isa. 55:1–2) Jesus doesn't call us to a self-improvement plan. Instead, He appeals to our deep thirsts and desires, even if we don't recognize it. Many people who want to follow Christ view Christianity as nothing more than an invitation to live a good moral life and believe in a finite set of certain doctrines. Few of us connect our relationship with Jesus to a life of passionate desire and fullness. Why have we concluded this? And why are so many men so desperately out of touch with their thirsts and desires?

Micah was the poster child for men who have disconnected from the thirst in their souls. He was in his early forties, had never married, and was deeply involved in his church's inner-city ministry. Though he had earned two graduate degrees in theology and in fine arts, he worked full-time as a telephone customer service rep so he could have "more flexibility for the ministry." In his spare time he ran several marathons a year. So I was more than a little intrigued when he told me he wanted to meet so he could understand why he was so undisciplined.

Not only was he disconnected from his deep thirst, but he had also developed a theological justification for his austere lifestyle of self-denial. "I really don't want anything and really don't need others," he noted in one of our first conversations. "As a Christian, I am here to serve others and meet their needs." And I didn't question his sincerity. But for many years Micah had neglected his own needs at the expense of his well-being. And there was one other problem: he was trapped in habitual compulsive masturbation. For decades he had prayed, begging God for more discipline. His compulsion had left him with a sense of failure, shame, and inadequacy. This was the one issue in his life that self-discipline could not touch.

## WHAT ARE YOU THIRSTY *FOR*?

If Thomas Aquinas's words are true—that every sinful behavior is rooted in a legitimate God-given appetite—then identifying those God-given longings must be our first order of business. Ask a man his longings and you might get a blank look—or one filled with fear. We've been told to repress our longings. To help men get in touch with their longings, I have led men through an exercise that helps them discover their deep thirsts and desires. While simple, it has proven quite revolutionary in helping men discover the language of their soul—a language in which every man must become fluent if he wants his soul to be free.

Initially, I ask men to identify and write out fifty deep thirsts or longings in their hearts. Most men, however, don't even have a category for thinking about such a question. "Do you mean, what are my goals?" they ask. Or, "Do you mean, what is my five-year plan?" Or, "Oh, right, yes! I want to take my wife on a nice trip for our anniversary—that's what I desire." Though these are legitimate desires, they aren't the deep desires that Jesus referred to in John 7.

When Micah did this exercise, he recognized how cut off he was from his desires and thirsts. Over time he was able to identify several core longings that he had suppressed in order to avoid pain and disappointment. In high school, Micah fell big-time for a blue-eyed soprano he knew in choir. They dated all through their senior year. When she broke up with him just after graduation, his heart was crushed. He compared the breakup to being sucker-punched in the gut and having the emotional wind knocked out of him.

Bruised, he eventually moved on and pursued a path in college leading him toward a career in vocal performance. At the beginning of his junior year, however, a new department chair took over. This man told Micah in no uncertain terms that he should change his major and give up the dream of performing professionally. Suddenly, every door to pursuing his passion had closed on him. Micah vowed he would never be disappointed like that again. So he disowned his desire. He developed spiritual aposia and convinced himself that his soul wasn't thirsty. But as he began to connect the dots of his story, Micah realized that he wouldn't find freedom from masturbation by becoming more disciplined. He could only break free as a result of the restoration of his heart.

"One of the first things God does as he restores a man," wrote John Eldredge, "is to reawaken desire."[2] The first major step in Micah's healing was the reawakening of the thirsts, longings, and desires that he had shut down years before. He recognized that his self-sufficiency and dedication to helping others was a self-protective strategy that prevented him from being hurt or rejected. His dedication to service allowed him to be affirmed and valued without taking the risk of being hurt in a relationship.

Masturbation was the only outlet in his life that came close to meeting his legitimate needs. As he recognized and understood more of the thirst and longing beneath that struggle, his desire for relationship and connection reawakened. Slowly, he realized he needed relationships to be a two-way street, not one-sided ministry to others. His heart awakened to the possibility of engaging in a relationship with a woman. His soul started coming alive.

## NAME YOUR THIRST

Whenever I ask a man to make a list of what his soul is thirsty for, I may as well be speaking Cantonese. Early in my own healing journey, my counselor encouraged me to talk about my longings. It was like trying to describe gravity. So to give men a place to start, I explain that people generally share seven core thirsts. Though this list is not exhaustive, it offers a straightforward way for you to begin to put words to what lies below the surface of your life:

- Attention—I long for people to like me. I long for your embrace.
- Affection—I long to be enjoyed. I long to be delighted in. I long for you to take pleasure in who I am.
- Affirmation—I long to know I have what it takes. I long for your blessing.

- Acceptance—I long to belong. I long to be desired.
- Satisfaction—I long for fullness. I long for well-being.
- Significance—I long for impact. I long for meaning. I long to be powerful.
- Security—I long to know I will be okay.

All of these core thirsts are God-given appetites and longings. When they are suppressed, cut off, or shut down, we resemble an Indy car running on four cylinders. Because of this, we fail to live from our hearts. To run on eight cylinders, we need to acknowledge that we are thirsty and identify what our thirsts are. Why? Because only when we identify them will we begin moving toward those desires according to God's design.

Once you have identified your deepest desires, you can begin understanding why pornography is so alluring. You can see beyond the easy rationale of your body's libido to the underlying longings of your soul. The sexual images and experiences you crave represent the fulfillment of one or more of your seven core thirsts: to be seen and valued, to feel affection and love, to be affirmed in your manliness and desirability, and so on—or at least they offer the illusion of all this in the moment.

## LUST IS THE OUTCOME OF DISORDERED DESIRE

After counseling people for more than twenty years, I'm convinced that there are only two kinds of people in the world: people who eat chocolate cake for breakfast and wish they hadn't, and people who shudder at the thought of chocolate cake for breakfast but should probably try it. In other words, there are those of us who demand that our desires be satisfied, and those who disown our desires.

Speaking to that second crowd, no doubt, Jesus addressed the issue of lust. "You have heard that it was said, 'Do not commit adultery.' But I tell you that anyone who looks at a woman lustfully has already committed adultery with her in his heart" (Matt. 5:27–28). The Greek word for "lust" in that passage is *epithumeo*, which means "to set the heart upon" or to "intensely desire."

Yet when Luke recorded Jesus' words as He broke bread with His twelve disciples at the Last Supper—"I have *earnestly desired* to eat this Passover with you before I suffer" (Luke 22:15 ESV, emphasis added)—he used the same word, *epithumeo*, that Jesus used to describe lust. Was Jesus lusting? Yes. Was Jesus sinning? Of course not. He was deeply in touch with the deep and godly desires in His heart.

Through the centuries, theologians and philosophers have referred to lust as disordered desire. Such a definition is extremely helpful in understanding Jesus' two uses of the word for lust, as well as clearing up our own misunderstandings. Disordered desire results from desires that are disowned, demanded, or misplaced

*Disowned* desire usually results from shame or pain. In high school, I told my Young Life leader that I was fervently praying, asking God to take away my sexual desires. They were just too strong. I actually thought God would be pleased if I became sexually neutered until I got married someday. With great wisdom and grace, my leader assured me that my sexual desires were a gift from God. To me they felt more like a curse; not unlike the feeling described by Frederick Buechner in his novel *Godric*: "Lust is the ape that gibbers in our loins. Tame him as we will by day, he rages all the wilder in our dreams by night. Just when we think we're safe from him, he raises up his ugly head and smirks, and there's no river in the world flows cold and strong enough to strike him down. Almighty God, why dost thou deck men out with such a loathsome toy?"[3]

Ambivalence over what feels like a loathsome toy of desire is a primary way that many men disown their sexual urges. Over the years, countless men have described to me their sexual desires as a part of them for which they feel both gratitude and contempt. They find it refreshing, then, when they learn that their desires are not too strong, but too little. C. S. Lewis hit the bull's-eye: "Our Lord finds our desires, not too strong, but too weak. We are half-hearted creatures, fooling about with drink and sex and ambition when infinite joy is offered us, like an ignorant child who wants to go on making mud pies in a slum because he cannot imagine what is meant by the offer of a holiday at the sea. We are far too easily pleased."[4]

While we try to ratchet down our desires, God invites us to desire even more deeply. But as Lewis wrote, we are far too easily pleased. Do you believe in your heart of hearts that when you indulge in porn, fantasy, or masturbation, your desires are actually *too weak?* If we truly believed it, perhaps we would stop trying to deny or suppress our desires and instead let them lead us to what our heart really longs for.

The problem with lust is that we've thrown the baby out with the bathwater.

Think about it this way. Suppose you have just finished a hard day of cycling or hiking in the heat of summer. Extremely thirsty, you return to your vehicle and grab the water bottle you packed earlier that morning. You are aware that the water in your container is comprised of countless molecules, each containing two hydrogen atoms and one oxygen atom. For some reason, you decide that you will only swallow the oxygen atoms and not the hydrogen atoms. Despite your best efforts, you can't do it because the two hydrogen atoms and the one oxygen atom cannot be separated. To separate them would mean you would no longer be drinking water, but something else. A man trying to suppress his lust is like someone trying to drink only the oxygen atoms.

*Demanded* desire is the opposite of disowned desire because we demand relief from the pain of unmet thirst. As broken and self-sufficient men, we reflexively seek relief for our unmet thirsts by moving in a direction away from God. God described it this way: "My people have committed two sins: They have forsaken me, the spring of living water, and have dug their own cisterns, broken cisterns that cannot hold water" (Jer. 2:13).

Longing for the comfort of being held in a woman's arms is quite different from demanding that comfort. When we demand that our desires be satisfied, we turn people into objects and end up using them—at cost to our own souls and the woman's dignity. When we demand, we leave no room for love because we go from being lovers to consumers.

A man compulsively drawn to porn does not have a problem with his desire. God created him with a natural attraction to feminine beauty. The problem is not that he is thirsty but that his desire has become a demand. Like something sipped from a funnel, whatever we turn to for the satisfaction of our thirsts will leak if it lies outside the scope of God's good gifts. So we return to the funnel again and again.

In our world today, if you want a movie, song, or video, you just press a button on one of your many hi-tech devices and—voilà!—there it is, on demand. But our souls weren't designed to work this way. In fact, in *The Great Divorce*, C. S. Lewis described *hell* as a place where people have no needs because they can get whatever they want just by imagining it—on demand![5]

Disordered desire can also be *misplaced*. When we misplace our desires, we direct our hearts toward something that takes the place of God's good gifts. It's the craving for ice cream when you feel depressed or the lust for porn when you are lonely. Larry Crabb explained it well: "When pleasures of any kind are used to satisfy (or at least to quiet) our crucial longings, then the craving for what only God can provide becomes a demanding tyrant driving us toward whatever relief is available. Our god becomes our appetite. Crucial longings meant to create a panting after God energize our addiction to whatever feels good for a moment."[6]

## WHY DOES YOUR FIRE BURN OUTSIDE THE FIREPLACE?

Over the years I've heard sermons and messages comparing our sexual desires to a fire burning in a fireplace. When the fire burns within the fireplace, it represents sexual desires within God's boundaries and design. Here it can be pleasurable and life giving. When the fire burns outside of the fireplace, it represents sexual desires expressed outside of God's boundaries and design. In this case, it causes damage and destruction.

I've never heard a sermon, however, that substantively addresses the issue of *why* the fire burns outside the fireplace. What causes the fire to burn out of control? What fuels the fire? To say that sin fuels the fire might be true, but something else in addition to sin must be addressed.

A close friend owns a ranch in the high country of Colorado. About seven years ago, the entire region, including his ranch, was infested with pine beetles, a perennial killer of forests. With so many trees infested, damaged, or dying, the ranch was at very high risk for a catastrophic wildfire. After lengthy consultations with forestry experts, he decided that the best long-term solution was to cut down every dead or infested tree. At tremendous cost and after countless hours of labor, his ranch no longer faces the threat of a wildfire. Hundreds of acres of mountainside are now bare, yet new life is beginning to emerge. And when the wildfire season begins, any neighboring flames will have nothing to consume.

Certain conditions make pine trees vulnerable: poor growing conditions, drought, fire damage, and root disease. Spiritually, our souls resemble that mountain forest. The interior forest of our souls is strong and vibrant. But like the trees on my friend's ranch, our souls can become dry, damaged, and vulnerable. Under certain conditions, the smallest spark of legitimate desire can ignite our vulnerable parts and burn far outside the fireplace of healthy, God-designed boundaries.

Can you identify the dead logs, broken branches, and dried-out parts of your soul? How has your soul experienced drought, root disease, or poor growing conditions? If you *don't* know the answers to these questions, I can almost guarantee that the fire of legitimate God-given desire will ignite your brokenness and burn outside of the fireplace with a ferocity that seems unstoppable.

If you know the answer—if you understand your brokenness—then your efforts to deforest the dead trees will create a fire line that prevents the wildfire of sexual passion from burning out of control. Coming to terms with our brokenness is a daunting process. But we must understand it in order to experience true freedom.

4

# Gathering the Broken Pieces

It's about the hole in the heart.
**—ADDICTION FOR DUMMIES**

Your inadequacy is your first qualification.
**—JOHN GAYNOR BANKS**

"What are you doing home so early?" my wife asked me as I walked through the front door.

"I decided to come home," I answered.

"But you just told me on the phone that you got called out on a job," she continued. The puzzled look on her face told me she wanted to know more.

I had called my wife to say I was working late. I wasn't. My scheme was to launch into my ritual of cruising for sex. But something made me change my mind. My wife was more than a little surprised when only twenty minutes later, I walked into our apartment.

"I said I *might* be working late." Now I was contradicting what I had actually said. This was the first time in as long as I could remember that I hadn't prepared an alibi. I was improvising my way forward.

"Either you got called out or you didn't. There's no maybe.

Which is it?" The emotional temperature in the room began to rise. My cheerful wife was suddenly on the offensive. The blood drained from my face and my mouth went dry.

"What I meant to say is—is—is that I would . . . be *home* late, but that I, I was le-leaving the office right then." I hoped that she wasn't noticing my perspiring forehead. "I had to take care of some things," I explained, praying she would let it go and change the subject.

"What *kind* of things did you have to take care of?" I had never been cross-examined in court, but I imagined this was close.

"I, uh, well . . . I, umm . . ." No intelligible words were coming from my mouth, but my flushed crimson appearance and throbbing heart betrayed me.

"Michael, what's going on?" There was no use continuing the charade. She caught me. The dam holding back the lies and deceit burst. "I didn't get called out," I mumbled.

"Then why did you say you did? What were you doing?"

After what seemed like hours of silence, I spoke the words my wife has dreaded ever since. "There is something I have to tell you . . ."

For the next several hours I poured out my secret life: porn, prostitutes, people and places she knew nothing about. To say Julianne was devastated would be an understatement. She was in shock, betrayed, confused, angry. I slept on the floor that night . . . and many nights following, as she cried herself to sleep behind a locked bedroom door.

July 10, 1994, was the worst day of my life. It was the day on which I unleashed a hurricane of destruction and was forced to watch the woman I loved crawl in the wreckage. When I was single, my actions didn't immediately affect anyone in my circle of family and friends. Now, the consequences of my recklessness could be seen in Julianne's eyes. I had caused my wife's worst nightmare to come true. Like a drunk driver, I was soaring over a steep cliff with my wife in the car, forced to watch her flail helplessly in slow motion without a seat belt before the inevitable crash.

July 10, 1994, was also the best day of my life. What made it so special? It was the day God threw open the door to freedom. Until then I had always been able to jump in the manure and come out smelling like a rose. Even when my addiction was nearly exposed in the newspaper years before, it hadn't broken me. I went to counseling, shared *most* of my struggle with friends, and read books. I always believed that I was eventually going to conquer the problem through my own effort. Yet I never actually came to the end of myself. But that day shattered me. I had reached the end of a dead-end road. I didn't understand how I had gotten there or how to find my way home.

Somehow that day, I managed to write these words in my journal:

> It has been three months since I've written in this journal. This might be the first honest entry I've ever made. Today has been the darkest day of my life. Julianne and I met with Larry regarding my sexual sin and adultery. Yes, adultery. I've brought destruction to the one I love. She's numb. She's devastated. I've decapitated the limbs of her soul and wounded her in the most vulnerable part of her heart. I've broken her trust and mocked my wedding vows. Today . . . I am helpless. Powerless. Defenseless. I'm incapable right now of bringing an ounce of joy to her life. I'm utterly incapable of changing, healing, or transforming my own life. Promises are empty. I am empty. I can't fix this. I can't fix me. I need the Gospel. God have mercy on me.

To paraphrase Richard Rohr, it is only through the holes in our soul that we break out and God breaks through.[1] Little did I know that this experience of profound brokenness was precisely what I needed for God to break through and do His most powerful work in me. For that to happen, I needed to come face-to-face with just how broken I was.

That summer I began to realize that my inner world was like the beetle-infested trees on my friend's ranch. Despite choosing to follow Jesus years before, I discovered that the roots of my soul were entangled and diseased, and had only known droughtlike growing conditions. Being that I was so spiritually and emotionally unhealthy, it's no wonder that any spark of God-given desire could cause a forest fire of sexual passion to burn out of control.

## WE ARE BROKEN MEN WHO MUST LIVE FROM OUR BROKENNESS

Deep in our masculine souls, we suspect that something is not quite right. Submerged below the surface, a part of us remains untouched and unaffected by our new life in Christ. This shouldn't come as a surprise. For many men, however, it is easier to attribute things not being quite right to a stretch of bad luck, not being at the top of their game, or needing an "engine tune-up" for their lives.

Our struggles with porn work the same way. We delay facing our problems, holding out for some point in the future when the issues simply evaporate or we discover the magic solution. We wonder if we are not doing something correctly, then determine that with enough effort we will figure out how to eliminate the trouble. But tell me, why do we need God if this is how we live? Only when we recognize the deeper rupture in our souls will we feel compelled to seek God with a passion that wells up from deep inside.

The fact is, we are broken men. Somewhere deep inside we sense the fracture in each of our souls, a fracture that encompasses our sinfulness and extends beyond it. Our hearts—the containers that hold love—are broken. That is why even when we drink deeply of God's living water, we are thirsty again. Like clay water jugs with cracked sides, we leak because we are broken.

Are you aware of all the things you can't put right on your own? Your lust? Your drivenness? Your anger? Your impatience? Your passivity? How you judge others? How money burns a hole in your pocket? How you like to drop names? What about the residue of shame you've carried for so long? Or the memories that haunt you? The private thoughts and fantasies no one else knows about?

For the first three years of my marriage, I harbored fantasies of being single. I loved my wife—as much as any sexually addicted poser could—but I resented being forced to consider anyone other than myself. Beneath my facade, nobody ever guessed that I regularly fantasized about Julianne dying, all so I would be free to pursue my dark version of personal happiness. Not knowing where my crazy daydreams were coming from, I often asked myself, "What *is* this?" It was brokenness. Between my own foolish choices and the way my life had shaped me, I was anything but whole.

As I've ministered to men over the years, one of the most frequent statements I hear is, "I want to be a man of integrity." Without question being a man of integrity should be a high priority for every man who wants to follow Jesus. But most of the time we think of integrity as exhibiting good morals, having strong character, and diligently obeying God's commands. Actually, these are all consequences of integrity. Integrity itself—taken from the Latin word *integer*—means to be *whole*. Just as a whole number is known as an *integer*, a whole man is known as a man of *integrity*. A man who is whole is a moral man and an obedient man. Each of these flows *from* integrity.

Only days after disclosing my double life to Julianne, I confided everything to my friend Dudley, including the lies I had told him. At the end of a hard conversation, he said to me, "Michael, you are one man with one life. The problem is that you've been living like several different men. I want, and God wants, you to become whole." His kind words described my brokenness but also pointed toward God's vision for me—to be whole.

King David was a man intimately acquainted with his brokenness. Aware of his divided heart, he wrote in the Psalms: "Train me, GOD, to walk straight; then I'll follow your true path. Put me together, one heart and mind; then, undivided, I'll worship in joyful fear" (86:11 MSG).

As a man heals from his bondage to porn, he *must* understand his brokenness and allow it to compel him toward Jesus. Our brokenness is our only requirement for receiving God's grace.

## OUR BEHAVIOR IS JUST THE TIP OF THE ICEBERG

Jesus taught that adultery and sexual immorality come out of the heart (Matt. 15:19). But what does this mean? In his classic book *Inside Out*, Larry Crabb compares our inner world to an iceberg. The visible tip of the iceberg represents our behaviors, conscious thoughts, and feelings—things people see and feel. The iceberg mass below the waterline represents those things that cannot be readily identified. These include motives, purposes, and attitudes of the heart, as well as painful memories and hidden emotions.[2] It doesn't take much to realize that a person can appear morally obedient, spiritually mature, and emotionally whole, yet below the waterline remain self-centered and immature. It is below the waterline, however, in the place of our inmost being, where the gospel is meant to transform us.

In the waters of our soul, something more deeply rooted must be addressed. But what is it? When Jesus taught that adultery and sexual immorality came out of the heart, He was not giving an anatomy lesson. In a heated conversation with the religious professionals of the day, Jesus had been discussing what makes a person clean or unclean. The popular teaching was that a person was unclean for not having followed certain ceremonial steps. But Jesus turned this teaching upside down. "What goes into a man's mouth does not make him 'unclean,'" Jesus said, "but what comes out of his mouth, that is what makes him 'unclean'" (Matt. 15:11). His point was that no matter how many acts of obedience we perform, our problems are internal, not external. Our actions and behavior—what comes out of us—are just the tip of the iceberg.

As if Jesus' impassioned discussion with the religious rule-keepers were not enough, He went on to utter His harshest words yet, to those who believed that God should be impressed with their moral performances. "Woe to you, teachers of the law and Pharisees, you hypocrites! You clean the outside of the cup and dish, but inside they are full of greed and self-indulgence. . . . First clean the inside of the cup and dish, and then the outside also will be clean" (Matt. 23:25–26).

What this means for a man caught in the chains of porn and lust is crucial. If you could somehow magically stop looking at porn and exercise self-control in place of lust, you still wouldn't be dealing with the problem below the waterline. You've only cleaned the outside of the cup and dish.

"The purposes of a person's heart are deep waters," wrote Solomon (Prov. 20:5 UPDATED NIV). Our hearts hold deep reasons for why we do what we do, which explains why our sinful actions and self-sufficient behaviors can make sense—at least internally. As discussed in the previous chapter, we are thirsty, but we often move in the wrong directions to satisfy our thirst. "This only have I found," wrote the author of Ecclesiastes. "God made mankind upright, but men have gone in search of many schemes" (7:29). Beneath the waterline we are driven by hidden agendas, unconscious goals, and ungodly passions—schemes to slake the thirst that God alone can quench.

Connecting these deep passions and purposes below the waterline to the behaviors, struggles, and issues above the waterline helps us recognize the cause of our confusing behavior. Understanding ourselves at this level is not about the "what" of our sin (*I can't stop looking at porn*), but the "why" (*porn promises to meet some need in me*).

The whys that explain our addictions can be categorized into four interwoven, underlying dimensions: *wickedness, weaknesses, woundedness*, and *warfare*.

## OUR BROKENNESS BEGINS WITH OUR WICKEDNESS

What comes to your mind when you hear the word *wickedness*? Adolf Hitler's concentration camps? Osama bin Laden's acts of terror? Serial killers? At the risk of sounding like a fire-and-brimstone evangelist, I need to emphasize here how wickedness serves as the foundation for all brokenness. Scripturally, wickedness involves a self-centered defiance of God. From Adam and Eve taking the forbidden fruit, to my own self-centered adultery, wickedness plays out as we turn away from God and become the captains of our own souls. As Isaiah wrote, "We all, like sheep, have gone astray, each of us has turned to his own way" (53:6). Any honest appraisal of our lives allows us to see that wickedness dwells in all of us.

Thankfully, wickedness does not complete the picture. Yes, we have a very active sin nature, but there's more to the picture than our inner world of sin. Most of us realize that in addition to wickedness, something else lurks in the shadow of our sinful choices. Our wickedness shapes how we respond to our weaknesses and woundedness.

## OUR BROKENNESS ACCENTUATES
## OUR WEAKNESS

*Weakness*—just hearing the word makes many of us uncomfortable. From the Protestant work ethic to health clubs to Viagra, our personal and cultural DNA sets itself against weakness. Weakness reminds us that we are vulnerable and dependent. It exposes our limitations, our shortcomings, our failures and imperfections. Weakness can leave us feeling helpless, powerless, impotent. In a culture that glorifies strength and independence, weakness is an obstacle to the good life.

Every man wants to appear strong, competent, and together—anything but weak. But no *actual* man, including Jesus, has ever lived without significant weakness. So what do we do? We fake it 'til we make it. We turn on the bravado. Develop a persona. Or we simply avoid any kind of risk. All of these reactions can set the stage for the compulsive pursuit of porn.

I've avoided risk most of my life. Recently I felt convicted about playing it safe in an effort to conceal a weakness. Living in Colorado, many of my friends love to camp, backpack, and rock climb. Though I've always felt drawn to such wilderness activities, I have systematically avoided them. *I don't have time . . . I don't have the equipment . . . It's too expensive . . . I'm too out of shape . . . I'll do it someday*, I convinced myself. In reality, I didn't pursue them because I felt tremendously inadequate and incompetent. Put me behind a podium or teaching in a classroom where I feel competent, but don't throw me into a group of men, send me into the woods, and ask me to be dependent. No thanks. I'll pass.

Recently my junior high son joined a competitive mountain-biking team. He has traveled throughout Colorado to ride and train on some of the most breathtaking trails in the United States. Little did I know that fathers are encouraged to participate with their sons. So suddenly, my very own flesh and bone, for whom I always want to appear strong, is inviting me to engage his passion by doing the very thing that makes me feel inadequate. I am faced with a choice. I can live by fear and continue to avoid what makes me feel inadequate. By doing this I will cheat myself and my son of some irreplaceable moments. Or I can humble myself; acknowledge my lack of experience, knowledge, and even proper equipment; and ask for help. I can seek out men to mentor and teach me everything I think I'm supposed to know. In doing so, my weakness could be transformed. By receiving the benefit of other men's wisdom, I could know the joy of pursuing adventure with other men.

In the days of my sexual addiction, I avoided any opportunity—including moving toward a woman with strength—that might expose my weakness. Today, I continue to learn what it means to move toward my inadequacy instead of away from it. It's not an easy thing, but God is faithful. Before becoming a Christian, the apostle Paul was incredibly driven, strong, and successful. In order for Paul to open his heart to Christ, God had to stop Paul in his tracks. On the road to Damascus, God temporarily blinded him (Acts 9). Immediately, this self-reliant man was forced to depend on God and others in a way he probably never had before.

In 2 Corinthians 12, Paul described another weakness—his "thorn in [the] flesh." Though we don't know the identity of this metaphorical thorn, his description sounds like physical suffering. Three times he cried out to God, "Take this away!" Yet God continued to respond, "My grace is all you need. My power works best in weakness" (v. 9 NLT).

God seems to have a special fondness for weakness because it is the doorway by which we enter His power. Through surrendered weakness, we discover that we really do need other people and God. We discover that God is a necessity, not just a luxury. So while men typically avoid facing their weakness, embracing it actually acts as a doorway to God's power.

## OUR BROKENNESS ENCOMPASSES OUR WOUNDEDNESS

A number of authors have aptly called sexual addiction a disorder of intimacy. There are at least two reasons why a man might have such a condition. One is that intimacy was never modeled and he is lacking in skill. More commonly, though, intimacy has proven painful and been a source of wounding.

Whenever I work with a man during a soul care intensive, I begin by asking him to fill out a detailed personal history. One form takes an inventory of any wounds he might have experienced during his formative years. He is asked to answer questions regarding physical, emotional, sexual, and spiritual wounding and abuse. It's uncanny how so many men complete the entire inventory but leave the wound section blank. Dozens of men have crossed this section out, or written "N/A" to indicate that the questions were not applicable to them. But then, as I listen to their stories, my heart breaks:

- the man who, at the age of thirteen, discovered his father's body just after he'd committed suicide
- the man who was sexually fondled by his scoutmaster
- the man who, on the first day of kindergarten, learned that both his parents were killed in a car accident on their way to pick him up after school
- the man whose father was a beloved deacon at church but regularly raged at the kids and hit his wife
- the man who was teased and bullied through junior high because he wore orthopedic braces on his legs
- the man whose father told him about sex by handing him a box of condoms and telling him to be sure he didn't get a girl pregnant

All these men initially reported to me that they didn't have any wounds. *Not applicable. Not me. I'm good.* None of them intentionally lied or tried to be deceitful. They had simply cut off that part of themselves in order to survive. The problem, however, is that the survival techniques that helped us go on when we were young prevent us from thriving when we are adults. Our solution becomes the problem.

Until we realize that we are wounded, we will never recognize how we turn to porn as a balm to heal the injuries of our hearts. As men we can admit our wickedness and perhaps our weakness, but our woundedness touches something too deep, too tender. Our culture tells us that men should be strong and resistant, unaffected and unmoved by pain. Acknowledging our woundedness feels like a betrayal of our masculinity. But exactly the opposite is true.

Jesus is our role model when it comes to handling woundedness. Among His many names and descriptions in the Bible, Jesus is called the Great Physician (based on Mark 2:17). During His three years of ministry, His mission consisted of preaching the good news of the kingdom, casting out demons, and healing the sick (Matt. 4:23–24).

Why, then, do we so often limit Jesus' ministry to forgiveness and payment for sin? His death on the cross restored our relationship with God and enabled us to receive eternal life in heaven. But the restoration of our relationship with God also makes restoration possible *in us.* Eternal life doesn't begin after we die—it begins right now. Just as Jesus' crucifixion shows us the merciful heart of God, Jesus' miraculous healings also reveal God's gracious heart—He is a God who restores and makes all things new (Rev. 21:5).

Throughout Scripture, God promises healing:

- "I am the LORD, your healer" (Ex. 15:26 ESV).
- "I will restore you to health and heal your wounds" (Jer. 30:17).

- "I will bring health and healing . . . I will heal my people" (Jer. 33:6).

A man's soul can be wounded in two ways. *Wounds of presence* are sins of commission—intentional or unintentional acts that never should have occurred but have caused hurt and damage. *Wounds of absence* are sins of omission—hurtful or damaging acts that occurred because something wasn't done (like neglect or abandonment).

Some wounds aren't the result of a specific event but the slow accumulation of disappointments. It's not the two-by-four over the head that these men have trouble accepting as a wound; it's the drop-by-drop buildup of pain and sorrow that can erode our soul as well.

When beginning to face the real impact of their wounding experiences, many men feel the need to defend the person who caused the wound—especially if it was a parent or loved one. "It wasn't their fault," they tell me. But owning our wounds is not about blame: it's about accounting for the damage that has occurred. D. H. Lawrence wrote:

> I am not a mechanism, an assembly of various sections.
> And it is not because the mechanism is working wrongly, that
>     I am ill.
> I am ill because of wounds to the soul, to the deep
>     emotional self
> and the wounds to the soul take a long, long time, only time
>     can help
> And patience, and a certain difficult repentance.[3]

How beautiful it is when a man humbles himself before the cross and repents of his wickedness. How wonderful it is when a man entrusts his weakness to God. How glorious it is, however, when a man faces his wounds and surrenders them to God's redemptive purposes. Richard Rohr reminds us that pain that is not transformed becomes pain that is transmitted.[4] In other words, unless our wounds are healed, we will eventually pass on our unresolved pain to the ones we love. This can happen for generations.

## OUR BROKENNESS ATTRACTS THE ENEMY'S WARFARE

If wickedness is the foundation of all brokenness, then warfare is the thread that ties our brokenness together. In the battle against pornography, lust, and sexual sin, the conflict involves so much more than naked flesh. As we already discussed, it includes our wickedness, our weakness, and our woundedness. But we also battle evil forces that before the creation of the world made the destruction of faith, hope, and love their goal. By attacking a man's sexuality— an essential expression of God's nature—this goal is more easily accomplished. Satan and his underlings hate your soul because of the light and life within you. Referring to Satan and his dark angels, Paul wrote that "our struggle is not against flesh and blood, but against the rulers, against the authorities, against the powers of this dark world and against the spiritual forces of evil in the heavenly realms" (Eph. 6:12).

In the embers of your wickedness, weakness, and woundedness, the Enemy lurks, seeking to throw gas on the fires of brokenness. In contrast to Jesus the Christ, who came to offer life, our Enemy came to steal, kill, and destroy your soul (John 10:10). He prowls around like a roaring lion seeking to devour you (1 Peter 5:8). He is the father of lies, our accuser (Job 1:6–11; Rev. 12:10). One of his most formidable weapons is deception. If the Enemy can convince you to believe his lies, then he can squelch whatever truth could set you free. (In chapter 9 I will focus more deeply on the reality of this invisible battle.)

## SURRENDERING OUR BROKENNESS

The greatest barrier to the life of freedom that God desires for us is not our brokenness. It is brokenness unsurrendered. When we conceal or refuse to surrender our wickedness, weakness, and woundedness, they remain not only out of sight but also out of the realm of healing.

Surrendering means more than "letting go and letting God." It means saying yes to God's ongoing invitation to come closer, to see Him as He really is. Surrendering is one of the most profound expressions of trust in a God who, if not trustworthy and full of kindness, is asking us to do the absurd. Sam Keen wrote:

> Surrender is a risk no sane man can take.
> Sanity never surrendered is a burden no man may carry.
> God give me madness that does not destroy
> wisdom, responsibility, and love.[5]

In the person of Jesus Christ, the absurdity of surrender seems irrational, for there is nothing rational about the God who created sunsets and seascapes to reveal Himself to us in brokenness. But He did this for us. *This is the good news.*

In Jesus, God rescues us from wickedness. "You were dead because of your sins and because your sinful nature was not yet cut away," wrote the apostle Paul. "Then God made you alive with Christ, for he forgave all our sins. He canceled the record of the charges against us and took it away by nailing it to the cross" (Col. 2:13–14 NLT).

In Jesus, God reveals Himself to us in weakness. He entered the world as a baby, born to an unwed peasant teenager and cradled in a food trough. He lived as a homeless servant who washed the feet of His disciples. Then He died a criminal's death (Luke 23:32–33).

In Jesus, God heals our wounds: "by his wounds we are healed" (Isa. 53:5).

In Jesus, God has defeated the Enemy and his warfare: "In this way, he disarmed the spiritual rulers and authorities. He shamed them publicly by his victory over them on the cross" (Col. 2:15 NLT).

In Jesus, God became broken for us so that we might be made whole: "As they were eating, Jesus took some bread and blessed it. Then he broke it in pieces and gave it to the disciples, saying, 'Take it, for this is my body.' And he took a cup of wine and gave thanks to God for it. He gave it to them, and they all drank from it. And he said to them, 'This is my blood, which confirms the covenant between God and his people. It is poured out as a sacrifice for many'" (Mark 14:22–24 NLT).

What are the vulnerabilities, limitations, disadvantages, shortcomings, and imperfections that make up your brokenness? What have you done with the pain you have received and the wounds you bear?

5

# Exposing the Counterfeits

*Jesus only comes to us in our realities, not in our illusions.*
**—DR. EKIE KIKULE**

"Ha-*lo*, my friend! You like designer watches? I have all kind," the slick salesman asked in a thick Malaysian accent.

"I'm really just looking," I replied. "But do you by any chance have the Omega James Bond Limited Edition Seamaster 007?" Part of me wanted to see what it looked like, and part of me hoped he didn't have it, just so I could move on.

"I think I have dat. Be right back." Before I knew it, he had crossed the street and disappeared into a sea of bodies. Music blared, strings of colored lights flashed above, and the smell of Chinese food from hawker stalls hung heavy in the atmosphere at the open-air night market in the heart of Kuala Lumpur, the capital of Malaysia. After speaking and ministering to pastors all week, it was my last night in town.

If you've never been to a night market in Asia, you should add it to your bucket list. You will either thank me or send me angry e-mails. In addition to tourist goods representing local culture, every night market, no matter the city, has a line of standard wares. You'll see designer items from Gucci, Coach, and Calvin Klein—clothes, sunglasses, luggage, purses, and perfume. You'll find top-brand electronics, like

Apple and Sony. You'll see more cigarette lighters and pocketknives than you could possibly imagine. And finally, there are the watches. Everywhere you look are watches.

All of these items share one thing in common. They are 100 percent, certifiably counterfeit. And there I was, an American minister, standing on a curb in Asia, waiting for the knockoff watch salesman, who, I was convinced, had gone to get the police and have me handcuffed. But suddenly he reappeared through the crowd, carrying a small suitcase.

"I have Omega Seamaster, my friend! James Bond, 007, yes?" He opened the suitcase on a cement street divider. One look at the watch and my heart began to pound. It was a beautiful timepiece, and I wanted to put it on. I knew the watch was a counterfeit. He knew the watch was a counterfeit. But in our shared conspiracy we carried on the charade. I tried on the watch, but the band was too big. He removed two links and it fit like a glove.

"Omega very nice. Beautiful watch look very good on you."

We had not discussed price, but he beat me to the punch.

"Three hundred ringgit for this beautiful watch, sir," he offered. I immediately calculated the exchange rate from Malaysian ringgit to U.S. dollars. At that price it would cost me about ninety-five dollars—almost four thousand less than the original. After engaging in the mandatory bargaining, we agreed on a much lower price, and I became the proud owner of a counterfeit four-thousand-dollar watch.

Today that watch sits in the top drawer of my dresser. My heart no longer races when I see it. On the contrary, I get a sinking feeling as I'm reminded it's not the real thing. Nor does the watch work anymore. It stopped running after only two months. Just like that watch, porn presents itself as the real thing, when in actuality it is 100 percent counterfeit. And just like that watch, it never lives up to our expectations. Let me elaborate.

## ANOTHER SLICK SALESMAN

In Luke 4, when Jesus was tempted by Satan, He refused three counterfeit offers that were made in an attempt to derail Him from His mission:

- "Jesus, full of the Holy Spirit, returned from the Jordan and was led by the Spirit in the desert, where for forty days he was tempted by the devil. He ate nothing during those days, and at the end of them he was hungry. The devil said to him, 'If you are the Son of God, tell this stone to become bread.' Jesus answered, 'It is written: "Man does not live on bread alone"'" (vv. 1–4). The first sales pitch Jesus heard was an appeal to turn to a *counterfeit good*. Jesus had not eaten for more than a month. His obvious weakness was His hunger. So what did the Enemy use as a target? He aimed straight for Jesus' legitimate desire: sustenance—*Tell this stone to become bread.*

- "The devil led him up to a high place and showed him in an instant all the kingdoms of the world. And he said to him, 'I will give you all their authority and splendor, for it has been given to me, and I can give it to anyone I want to. So if you worship me, it will all be yours.' Jesus answered, 'It is written: "Worship the Lord your God and serve him only"'" (vv. 5–8). The second sales pitch Jesus heard was an appeal to *counterfeit worship*. Satan wants you to worship an idol instead of God. One of Satan's basic strategies is saying, *All of this can be yours, if* . . .

- "The devil led him to Jerusalem and had him stand on the highest point of the temple. 'If you are the Son of

God,' he said, 'throw yourself down from here. For it is written: "He will command his angels concerning you to guard you carefully; they will lift you up in their hands, so that you will not strike your foot against a stone."' Jesus answered, 'It says: "Do not put the Lord your God to the test"'" (vv. 9–12). The third sales pitch was an appeal to a *counterfeit truth*. Satan strategically quoted Scripture, but used it in a way that would cause Jesus' destruction. *If You throw yourself down, God will rescue You.*

This explains why porn is such a snare to our souls. It sells us a pack of lies by making us feel so alive . . . for a moment. But the "life" it hawks is 180 degrees different from the life Jesus offers. Porn's "life" is a counterfeit, just like my Omega watch.

When struggling with bad fruit above ground (like addiction to porn and other behaviors springing from sexual brokenness), we must understand the hidden roots below the surface from which they grow. In my experience, the same three spiritual counterfeits lie at the root of the problem: counterfeit good, counterfeit truth, and counterfeit worship.

## COUNTERFEIT GOOD

For centuries, writers on Christian spirituality have taught on the "centered life." This means being connected to and living from the deep center of our beings, where God dwells. When we are truly centered, we know a deep sense of well-being, joy, and peace. In my experience, however, many more people talk about the centered life than live it. The reason for this is counterfeit good.

As I write this chapter, I am under a pressing deadline. It isn't surprising, then, that while writing in my office, I have experienced intense urges to go to Starbucks for an iced Venti Quad Skinny Vanilla Latte, walk across the parking lot to the nearby mall and window-shop, surf the Internet, take my wife out to lunch, write thank-you notes, check the *New York Times* on my iPhone, start reading the new Bonhoeffer biography on my bookshelf, and drive to the Apple Store and buy anything.

Notice that none of the things I listed are inherently bad, and some of them are quite admirable. What each of these shares in common is their remarkable ability to provide a counterfeit sense of being centered. Counterfeit good always appeals to a legitimate desire. Today, my legitimate desire is for peace and competence.

When the devil tempted Jesus to turn stones into bread, he was appealing to Jesus' legitimate desire for food. In the case of my knockoff watch, the legitimate desire was a longing for approval and acceptance, born out of my insecurity. With porn, any number of legitimate desires may fuel the lust—affection, comfort, strength, or affirmation.

It might help to compare *designer gifts* with *deceiver gifts*. Designer gifts are God's blessings and provision for our genuine needs as human beings, and our God-given desires and longings. For example, men naturally long for affirmation and affection from a real woman. God designed us that way. A real woman who offers us real sex and intimacy and calls us to step up to real manhood in the context of the everyday realities of life is a gift. Marriage, though not given to everyone, is one of our Designer's most satisfying gifts of grace.

But it's a *gift!* It stops being grace when we try to buy its perks for ourselves illegitimately . . . when we try to meet our own needs for acceptance and affirmation and affection on our own terms. He warns us that we're getting suckered by a counterfeit: "Don't be deceived, my dear brothers. Every good and perfect gift is from above, coming down from the Father of the heavenly lights, who does not change like shifting shadows" (James 1:16–17).

My friend Danny is passionate about baseball. He is also deeply committed to working on his soul—understanding his brokenness and walking with Jesus to be restored. In 2005 we drove together to the Colorado Rockies' opening day game. During our drive he shared that he hadn't missed an opening day game in years.

Through his involvement in a men's group, he realized that he "needed" to attend opening day the way an alcoholic needs a drink. Danny had recently discovered that opening day numbed the pain of growing up with an absent father because it symbolized the minimal time and attention his father gave him. His legitimate desire for fatherly involvement attached itself to a designer gift—a legitimate good.

But because attendance at opening day was an attempt to protect himself from the pain of his wound, the legitimate good became a counterfeit good. He was turning stones into bread. The game we attended was the first time his heart was free from the need to be there.

Every gift from our Designer has a corresponding gift from the deceiver—a "shadow" gift. And you can bet your three hundred ringgits that every deceiver gift is a counterfeit. Satan cannot create anything; he can only take what has been created and twist it against its design. So, we are tempted to overindulge the Designer's gift of food. We might make a god out of alcohol—turning to it addictively to meet all sorts of inner needs—or maybe we make a god out of *not* drinking alcohol. We are deceived into believing that deceiver gifts will actually make us flourish.

Jonah warned us that we cannot keep both the counterfeit and the real at the same time. We must choose. "Those who cling to worthless idols forfeit the grace that could be theirs," he wrote (2:8). Counterfeit worship renders us unable to receive God's good gifts. When the Israelites were fleeing from slavery toward true freedom in the promised land, they got fed up with God and his provision of manna, and threatened to return to the gods of Egypt—where they could enjoy leeks and onions . . . while living in bondage. Embracing the counterfeit meant forfeiting the real.

That's what porn and lust do to us. They tell us we're not going to receive God's provision, that we'll never be satisfied with His manna, so we're better off finding our own. But the intimacy we experience in those illicit moments is a counterfeit intimacy. It makes us feel like men without requiring us to *be* men—until we wake up one day with a cheap imitation of intimacy in our top drawer.

We begin our journey from slavery to freedom when we expose the counterfeits at the root of our brokenness and admit our thirst for the real thing. It involves shifting our focus from the external objects of temptation (i.e., women and porn) and, as I said earlier, taking an authentic look at the spiritual roots under the surface.

## COUNTERFEIT TRUTH

Not only can all of our intense urges provide a sense of counterfeit good; they can also provide us with a sense of counterfeit truth. The truth is that my stress level is significantly above average and any of the counterfeit goods mentioned earlier would allow me to escape, however momentarily, from the stress. At best, they put a Band-Aid on the problem. At worst, they create more stress through procrastination, overspending, or overconsuming.

Pornography, sexual compulsion, and sexual addiction allow us to escape from the painful realities in our lives—at least for a little while. Pascal wrote, "The way to render a man happy is to engage him with an object that will make him forget his private troubles."[1] If I'm feeling sad, rejected, lonely, or irritable, porn or lust will initially help me avoid dealing with those unpleasant feelings. Addictions are strategies we use to keep the truth from ourselves by blinding us from seeing what's true about us. They give us temporary permission to live in denial; they help us suppress inconvenient or uncomfortable truths. But the escape is not real, and it doesn't last. What our souls truly need and thirst for are freedom, transformation, and deliverance. And the only path down that road leads right through truth, according to Jesus: "If you hold to my teaching, you are really my disciples. Then you will know the truth, and the truth will set you free" (John 8:31–32).

## COUNTERFEIT WORSHIP

In *The Brothers Karamazov*, Fyodor Dostoyevsky wrote that no man can live without worshipping something.[2] This explains why God began the first of the Ten Commandments by reminding us that He is a jealous God who will not tolerate us having any other gods before Him. And then, in the second commandment He tells us not to worship idols (Ex. 20:3–4). Worship is reflexive to all of us. Whether you have been a Christian for decades or you're an atheist, in your heart, you worship something or someone. You may worship porn, sex, or feminine beauty. You may worship achievement, money, or reputation. You may worship food, material things, or people's approval. But everyone worships something.

Biblically, any counterfeit worship is considered idolatry. Idolatry is more than something people do in faraway cultures when they bow down to statues. "An idol," wrote Tim Keller, "is anything more important to you than God, anything that absorbs your heart and imagination more than God, anything you seek to give you what only God can give you."[3]

With rich, detailed imagery, Scripture describes our conflicted relationship to idols. For example, it says we are prone to make and turn to idols, set up idols in our hearts, lift up our souls to idols, serve and cling to idols, consult and boast in idols, and make sacrifices to them. Why is that so bad? Many reasons, but one in particular is that demonic spirits are attached to these idols (1 Cor. 10:20).

Scripture also warns that when we give ourselves to an idol, it ensnares and traps us so we cannot break free (Deut. 7:25). We are fooled into thinking an idol is serving us when in reality we are serving it. We have fallen for a counterfeit "god" to worship.

Unbelief lies at the heart of idolatry. Some well-meaning Christians might say, "I'm a believer, so unbelief is not a problem for me." But unbelief is rarely concerned with God's existence or whether we believe that Christianity is true. Instead, unbelief deals with God's character—is God trustworthy, and is He truly who He says He is?

In his classic book *The Knowledge of the Holy*, A. W. Tozer suggests that idolatry is asking the question, "What is God like?" and getting the wrong answer.[4] When we get the wrong answer to the question of what God is like, we take matters into our own hands. We turn to something or someone we believe will provide us with what our souls need, and before we even realize it, our worship becomes counterfeit because our new god is counterfeit. Tim Keller wrote: "A counterfeit god [idol] is anything so central and essential to your life that, should you lose it, your life would feel hardly worth living. . . . An idol has such a controlling position in your heart that you can spend most of your passion and energy, your emotional and financial resources, on it without a second thought."[5]

Of course, few of us would admit even to ourselves that porn has become an idol, at least not until we realize how central and essential it has become and the controlling power it exerts over us. Then we realize we are worshipping a counterfeit god.

Despite my struggles with lust and porn in my early years of following Christ, I intentionally devoted myself to practicing the Christian disciplines, especially memorizing Scripture. So to arm myself for the war against sexual temptation, I memorized 1 Corinthians 10:13: "No temptation has seized you except what is common to man. And God is faithful; he will not let you be tempted beyond what you can bear. But when you are tempted, he will also provide a way out so that you can stand up under it."

To a young man wrestling with sexual compulsions, the promise of not being tempted beyond what I could bear and being given a way of escape was incredibly good news. So why did I keep giving in to temptation with greater and greater frequency? Even with the verse etched in my mind and hidden in my heart, I wasn't experiencing God's way of escape, and my temptation certainly felt like more than I could bear.

Years later I realized that the next verse (which I didn't memorize or connect with temptation) was critical to understanding Paul's teaching on temptation: "Therefore, my dear friends, flee from idolatry" (v. 14). Paul drew a crucial link between our temptation and idolatry. If we're tempted with something from which we can't seem to break free, we can be pretty certain that it has become an idol in our hearts.

## SOMETHING TREASURED MUST DIE

You have probably heard this joke before. At first glance it just seems like a cute play on words, but there's more to it:

A preschool-age boy approaches his grandfather and asks, "Grandpa, will you make a sound like a frog?" The grandpa croaks like a frog. Again the child asks, "Grandpa, will you make a sound like a frog?" Once more, the grandfather croaks like a frog. After going back and forth like this for some time, the grandfather finally asks the young boy why he wanted to hear frog sounds. "Because," says the boy, "Grandma said that when you croak, we are all going to Disneyland."

Compulsive sexual sin, porn, and lust operate like our own little Disneyland—our Magic Kingdom—where we can escape our momentary struggles, pains, or boredom. But like the little boy who innocently believed he was just playing a game with his grandpa, we, too, fail to see the true cost of our journey to the "Magic Kingdom." The boy, preoccupied with getting mouse ears, is unaware that to obtain them, his beloved grandfather must die. It is the same for us when we become enslaved to illicit sex: we don't understand that to get it, something treasured must die; something valuable will be sacrificed. We addictively pursue our counterfeit Disneyland at the expense of some deeper longing, at the expense of those we love and care for. Or ultimately, at the expense of our own souls. Unmasking the counterfeits and exposing the deep needs, longings, and thirsts within us positions our hearts to draw life from the only place it is available—Christ.

## HOW IN THE WORLD DID I END UP HERE?

In your struggle with sexual compulsions, do you ever wonder how in the world you ended up where you are? I can pretty much guarantee that you didn't wake up one morning and consciously decide to get hooked. No, for most men, it's a subtle slide over time down a slippery slope, a slide that usually starts with an appeal to counterfeit worship. Notice how Paul described the journey as a series of transactions where something real is exchanged for something counterfeit:

> For although they knew God, they neither glorified him as God nor gave thanks to him, but their thinking became futile and their foolish hearts were darkened. Although they claimed to be wise, they became fools and exchanged the glory of the immortal God for images made to look like mortal man and birds and animals and reptiles.
>
> Therefore God gave them over in the sinful desires of their hearts to sexual impurity for the degrading of their bodies with

one another. They exchanged the truth of God for a lie, and worshiped and served created things rather than the Creator—who is forever praised. (Rom. 1:21–25)

Given our preoccupation with the images of pornography, it almost seems like Paul is writing to computer-savvy men in the twenty-first century. What we see is the progression of compulsion. It starts when we turn away from God as our source of life and turn other things into idols that we're convinced will satisfy our desires. We worship and serve "created things rather than the Creator"—that's counterfeit worship.

Along the way we try desperately to numb the painful realities in our lives—the discontent, disappointment, dashed dreams, or fears often going back decades and rarely related directly to sex. Rather than face what's really churning beneath the surface, we opt for denial and distraction in fantasy "relationships" that get us off the hook from stepping up to the plate as real men. Our minds become "futile . . . foolish . . . darkened"—that's counterfeit truth.

Last, we give up hope of ever satisfying the good desires in our hearts—the hope for genuine heart and soul connections, for authentic intimacy with God and people. We settle for gratifying "the sinful desires of [our] hearts" and "the degrading of [our] bodies"—that's counterfeit good.

It is never too late to trade our Asian knockoffs for the real thing. No matter how much you have already lost, there's still time to surrender the counterfeits in exchange for the real things. Again, Tim Keller has explained: "Idols cannot simply be removed. They must be replaced. If you only try to uproot them, they grow back; but they can be supplanted. By what? By God himself, of course. But by God we do not mean a general belief in his existence. Most people have that, yet their souls are riddled with idols. What we need is a living encounter with God."[6]

It is never too late to leave the Magic Kingdom of lust and step into the reality of God's kingdom. And it is never too late to exchange the false intimacy of images and illicit encounters for authentic relationships and God's gifts. A living encounter with God is the destination. But first, we need to explore the obstacles that stand in the way of such an encounter.

6

# Shame and Core Beliefs

It's a sad man who's living in his own skin
and can't stand the company.

**—BRUCE SPRINGSTEEN, "BETTER DAYS"**[1]

Rob walked into his supervisor's office for what he thought was a conversation about fixing a scheduling conflict with a major client. When his supervisor asked him to take a seat, he realized this conversation was going to be more serious.

"I need you to take a look at these," his boss said, clearing his throat as he pushed a half-inch stack of paper across the desk. He was caught totally off guard. Rob looked at the top page and immediately his face turned hot and his heart pounded like a bass drum in his chest. Slumping in the chair, he let out an expletive and sighed.

Staring back at him was over six months of Internet history exposing his porn use on the company computer. The proof before him was undeniable. Next Rob's boss pushed a copy of the company's Internet usage agreement across the desk, which explicitly prohibited viewing pornographic material during company time and on company computers. The agreement, bearing Rob's signature, stipulated immediate termination for anyone violating the policy. Numb, Rob walked out of his supervisor's office, emptied his desk, and joined the ranks of the unemployed—all because of porn.

The sting of Rob's shame ran deep. First, he felt the shame of looking at porn—the embarrassment at being caught, the humiliation of being fired from his job, and mortification at the thought of having to tell his wife that he was fired . . . and why.

But another shame ran deeper in Rob, a shame he had no idea was there. A shame that needed to be exposed if he was ever going to escape the endless cycle of lather, rinse, repeat that had held him captive for so long.

## THE DIFFERENCE BETWEEN SHAME AND GUILT

Understanding shame is crucial in our journey from lust and addiction to freedom. This can be especially confusing and complex in the church, where leaders and laypeople often use condemnation, judgment, and shame to motivate people toward "right behavior."

For starters, shame is often confused with guilt. Guilt is the conviction we feel when we have violated some standard, when we have *done wrong*. For instance, if a person lies, steals, or commits adultery, he will typically feel some sense of guilt for having *done wrong*. In Rob's case, he felt guilty for what he did and for the hurtful consequences that resulted. Scripture promises that our sin can lead us to God through the cross of Christ, where we can experience cleansing, forgiveness, and restoration (1 John 1:3–9).

But while guilt says, "I have *done* wrong," shame says, "I *am* wrong." Shame is a feeling (which quickly becomes a belief) that we are defective, flawed, bad, or worthless. The lens of shame always focuses not on what a person has *done* but on who the person *is*. It focuses on one's *self*. The heaviness and torment of shame are unbearable. And the verdict is always the same—that at our core we are inferior, inadequate, or unacceptable.

At this point you may be wondering, *But doesn't the Bible teach that we are worthless and that we are unacceptable?* Or maybe like so many men, you are asking, "As a Christian, isn't it *right* for me to feel shame?" These questions are crucial because how we answer them determines how we experience God. They also determine whether we experience the good news as good news, or *sort of* good news.

## IN THE BEGINNING, ADAM AND EVE WERE NAKED AND UNASHAMED

For clarity, let's go back to the garden of Eden, where shame first appeared. Before the entry of sin, Scripture tells us that "the man and his wife were both naked, and they felt no shame" (Gen. 2:25). This reference to nakedness suggests something much more than not wearing clothes. Naked and unashamed describes Adam and Eve's relationship with God and their relationship with each other. To be naked and unashamed *before* God meant that Adam and Eve were both free and able to offer to God exactly who they were, without holding anything back or hiding their true selves. They were fully known, just as they were created to be, and they were fully okay with that. This led to an uninhibited intimacy with God and with each other.

To be naked and unashamed *before each other* was a sacred proclamation of their unique soul identities as man and woman. It affirmed that the distinctions between the two of them were good. Up to this point, neither Adam nor Eve had experienced any self-consciousness in relation to their distinct personhood as man and woman. We can only speculate, but I don't think Adam ever wondered if he was a good lover or if his hairline was receding. In the same vein, I doubt Eve ever wondered if her ideas were as valuable as Adam's, if she was too fat, or if her breasts were the right size.

Another factor of being naked and unashamed was their freedom to offer themselves to each other as a kind of blessing. God said that it was not good for Adam to be alone (Gen. 2:18). So Eve was God's gift to Adam, just as Adam was God's gift to Eve. In humble confidence they would have offered themselves to each other, knowing that who they were and what they offered was more than just good enough—it was *very* good.

## THE EFFECTS OF SIN: HIDDENNESS AND SHAME

The effects of sin and shame, however, changed everything. When Adam and Eve reached beyond God's provision, the consequences were as swift as they were dramatic. The greatest of these changes concerned their hiddenness—first between the two of them, then between them and God. Even in the garden, shame's first words to Adam and Eve were, *You'd better go hide*: "Then the eyes of both of them were opened, and they realized they were naked; so they sewed fig leaves together and made coverings for themselves" (Gen. 3:7).

Here we see a reversal of Adam and Eve's relational blessings. Because Adam and Eve ate the fruit from the Tree of Knowledge of Good and Evil, their eyes were now opened. Their newly gained knowledge of good and evil made them keenly aware of their loss of innocence (Gen. 2:17). They went from being naked and unashamed to hiding and covering their true selves.

For the first time each turned away from the other's gaze. After all, if they could put their own wishes before God's, they must have realized they could also put their own welfare before each other's. How could Adam ever trust Eve again after she broke God's trust? And how could Eve trust Adam after he did the same?

Vulnerability, once a blessing, became a liability. Unity, once a reflection of God's nature, now divided them. Being known, once a gift, set them up for possible heartbreak. So they gathered fig leaves, not just to cover up physical nakedness but also to cover their nakedness of soul. Hiddenness became Adam and Eve's self-protective strategy of choice in relationships.

But hiddenness infected their intimacy with God as well: "Then the man and his wife heard the sound of the LORD God as he was walking in the garden in the cool of the day, and they hid from the LORD God among the trees of the garden. But the LORD God called to the man, 'Where are you?' He answered, 'I heard you in the garden, and I was afraid because I was naked; so I hid'" (Gen. 3:8–10).

Notice that God came walking in the cool of the day as if He was doing what He had always done—seeking out conversation with His kids. Without looking closely at the story, we might assume God came to the garden ready to kick some butt and dole out punishment. But actually God came looking for them, not primarily to punish or shame them but to engage with them. He wasn't trying to determine their location. He didn't need a GPS to lock in on their coordinates. God asked, "Where are you?" to determine the posture of their hearts. Would Adam and Eve humble themselves? Would they trust in His character? Would they believe that He was the same God that day as He had been on all of the previous days? Or would they believe the lie of the serpent, who insinuated that God really couldn't be trusted?

By hiding, Adam and Eve answered those questions. Suddenly Adam and Eve were afraid of God. Their shame became a barrier to His offer of mercy, love, and care. Between the fig leaves and running for cover in the trees, they removed themselves from being able to receive what only God could offer. Andrew Comiskey wrote, "Shame is the raincoat over the soul repelling the living water of Jesus that would otherwise establish us as the beloved of God."[2] Shame pushed them away from God instead of drawing them *to* God.

Just as our ancestors in the garden of Eden hid their shame beneath fig leaves, we invent modern-day fig leaves to hide our fundamental shame. Some men hide behind four-thousand-dollar watches and half-million-dollar sports cars. Others hide behind their theological knowledge, ministries, or positions of spiritual authority. Still others hide behind masks of superficiality, deadness, or intellectual dullness. I'm well acquainted with fig leaves too. For most of my life, humor and being a know-it-all have been my foliage of choice. Whatever fig leaves we choose, hiding our true selves goes against God's design for us. It's not natural, and it never leads to life.

## God Doesn't Shame Us

Nevertheless God pursues us, even in the face of our disobedience and broken trust. And He doesn't stop there. When Adam and Eve covered themselves with fig leaves, God made them garments of animal skin (Gen. 3:21). A living creature shed its blood and gave its life—foreshadowing the cross, where Jesus would shed His blood to cover our shame and wash away our guilt, thus making us comfortable again in God's presence. It's as if God said, "If you think fig leaves will take away your shame, you'd better think twice. Only I can take away your shame."

And that's exactly what He does. The liberating truth of the gospel is that through the blood of Jesus, we are forgiven and made clean. Even more, we belong to a God who does not shame us. He did not shame Adam and Eve. He may have asked for them to give an account of their actions (3:11, 13), but He did not shame them, and He does not shame you or me.

Just take a good look at Jesus, who is the visible image of the invisible God (Col. 1:15). He didn't shame sexually broken people. When He encountered a Samaritan woman with a history of failed relationships, He offered her a drink of living water. With all tenderness He explained that He knew she had been married five times and was living with her boyfriend—yet He chose to divulge His true identity to her instead of dousing her with shame (John 4). When Jesus encountered a woman caught in the act of adultery, He refused to condemn her (John 8). Jesus met prostitutes—women despised as outcasts—and loved them with a great purity (Luke 7:36–50). The sexual brokenness of others did not embarrass Jesus or put Him off. For the most broken people in Jewish society, Jesus extended mercy, forgiveness, and hope into their sexual messes.

This tells us that the voice of shame should never be confused with the voice of God. The voice of shame comes from our brokenness, not from our loving heavenly Father. God never turns away from our brokenness. But in regard to our shame, we have good news: "There is now no condemnation for those who are in Christ Jesus" (Rom. 8:1).

## HIDING THE BROKENNESS PROLONGS THE SHAME

Hiddenness affects our relationships in another way too—it prevents us from receiving love from the Father. If shame and hiddenness are the raincoat over the soul, then trying hard to be good enough is the impressive suit that convinces us we are loved. When we listen to the voice of shame, we begin believing the lie that our wickedness, weakness, and woundedness disqualify us from God's love.

But the opposite is true. Jesus proclaimed that God passionately desires to bind up the brokenhearted and set the captives free (Luke 4:18–19). But how can He transform our brokenness into wholeness when we insist on concealing it? When we hide, we limit God's ability to reveal and heal those parts of us that desperately need the touch of the Great Physician, the Wonderful Counselor, and the Comforter. When we desperately try to maintain our appearance, we end up delaying our rescue.

Since that fateful day in the garden of Eden, all of us have followed Adam and Eve's example by attempting to earn love. We believe that in order to be loved, we must perform. All of us develop a strategy or way of relating to our inner worlds that convinces us to feel that we are okay, that we are loved, that we are desired. To satisfy our thirst for love, we run toward broken cisterns that cannot hold water.

This performance approach, however, presents us with three problems. First, performance is a treadmill that never stops running. How can we know when at last we are good enough? How can we know that we are performing well enough? The man who derives his identity and seeks out love through performance, achievement, or trying to be good enough sets himself up to live with enormous pressure. Such an approach is wearisome. It exhausts the soul and prevents him from receiving all of the good things that God offers.

Second, the performance approach is rooted in pride—which is another word for self-sufficiency. The few who somehow meet their own performance standards see no need for the gospel. The rich young ruler in Mark 10:17 was such a man. He had followed God's commands. He performed well and looked good. His suit of performance cloaked his raincoat of shame. But despite all this, his question to Jesus revealed that he was still missing something. "Teacher, what [else] must I do to inherit eternal life?"

The man's question didn't concern just going to heaven when he died. He was asking about entering the kingdom of God and joining Jesus in building His kingdom. But Jesus knew his heart. When this man offered proof of his righteousness—keeping the Ten Commandments—Jesus revealed to him something that his self-sufficiency could not produce. He asked the man to go and sell everything he had and give it to the poor. The story tells us the man was very wealthy. He hung his head and walked away. Though he looked good on the outside, something inside wouldn't allow him to let go of his wealth. Perhaps he allowed his earthly treasure to define him and delude him into believing his value was based on his riches.

Finally, the performance approach leads to the development of a false self. Each of us creates a persona in hopes of convincing others that this is who we really are. It's our game face. Our best foot forward. Who we want to be in others' eyes.

In his novel *Too Late the Phalarope*, Alan Paton described a man with a dark sexual secret, whose false self led to public disgrace and imprisonment: "He was always two men. The one was the soldier of the war, with all the English ribbons that his father hated; the lieutenant in the police, second only to the captain; the great rugby player, hero of thousands of boys and men. The other was the dark and silent man, hiding from all men secret knowledge of himself, with that hardness and coldness that made men afraid of him, afraid even to speak to him."[3]

But, of course, all this hiding and performing and pretending prevents us from receiving what our hearts long for. A false self cannot be loved. A fake self does not exist; it is only illusion. You and I can only be loved for our true selves, as unlovable as we think we might be.

## WHAT ARE YOUR CORE BELIEFS?

When my son was four, he went through a Batman phase, which meant he often wore his Batman T-shirt. One day when we walked into the Home Depot, an enthusiastic salesperson greeted my son with the words, "Hi, Batman!" Reflexively, CJ turned to me and exclaimed, "Dad, he knows my true identity!" To recover your heart from the chains of lust and porn, nothing is more important than discovering your true identity.

But chances are, you don't know your true identity. Most likely, you either define yourself by your shame and you know it, or you define yourself by performing well without realizing the shame lurking beneath the surface. Both are nothing more than a false identity. Of course, you may live from a deep truth within you that aligns with God's truth about who you are. But I've met very few people who live with that kind of clarity deep in their souls. What a man believes intellectually, theologically, and doctrinally very rarely resembles what he believes about himself—and about God—deep in his soul.

In decades of clinical work with thousands of sexually compulsive men, Patrick Carnes identified a pattern of four core beliefs that are deeply embedded in the internal belief structure of sex addicts prior to engaging in the addiction.[4] Whether a man struggling with porn is a sex addict in the truest sense, or something less than that, the following beliefs are in operation.

- *I Am Basically a Bad/Unworthy Person*

    Men with sexually compulsive behavior patterns typically believe they are somehow bad or unworthy. They see themselves through the lens of worthlessness. "Nice Christian guys" tend to voice this shame-based belief more in terms of not being okay, not being good enough, not measuring up, or somehow being different. The semantics are less important than the realization that their core beliefs are based on shame.

- *Nobody Would Love Me as I Am*

    Men with sexual compulsions deeply believe that nobody would love them for who they are. Since early childhood, many of these men experienced wounds of abuse or neglect. As a result, love never took root in their souls. Some may have had positive experiences of being loved, but in their closest relationships they encountered rejection, abandonment, judgment, or shame, which convinced them that they truly are unlovable. As with the previous core belief, some men do not identify with the exact wording "Nobody would love me as I am"; they believe instead "If people really knew me they wouldn't want me."

- *I Can't Get My Needs Met by Depending on Others*

  Men with sexual compulsions tend to believe that if their needs are going to be met, it's up to them to meet them. When speaking of needs, I'm not referring to the basic needs of food, clothing, and shelter. I'm referring here to soul cravings, such as the desire for affection, intimacy, or acceptance.

- *Sex Is My Most Important Need*

  Men with sexual compulsions assume that sex is their most important need. For these men, sex is the only way they know how to experience intimacy. Lust and porn represent the promise of meeting some other deep need for which their souls are thirsty.

  So when I speak with men about the fourth core belief, I often ask them to fill in the blank in this sentence: "_____ is my most important need." Some men answer that their most important need is feminine affirmation. Some answer that they need the affection of a woman. Others answer that they need the acceptance of a woman—all of which lust and sexual acting out provide. So really, their most important need isn't sex. They're looking for affirmation, acceptance, and approval, all from a woman.

So how do we begin identifying our true beliefs about ourselves? First, misguided core beliefs are formed early in life, and they are always formed in our brokenness. If you want to identify what your core beliefs are, just look at your brokenness. What are your wounds and weaknesses? They will become the place where the lies of the Enemy become your beliefs. That will also become the place where you take matters into your own hands to overcome weakness or find relief for the pain of the wound. Put simply, we hide, compensate for, or seek relief from our wounds and weaknesses. Our brokenness is also the place where we become vulnerable to the Enemy's lies.

## HOW TO OVERCOME YOUR SHAME

### Begin by Pulling Back the Curtain

In the movie classic *The Wizard of Oz*, Dorothy, the Scarecrow, the Tin Man, and the Cowardly Lion finally reach the Emerald City in hopes that the Wizard can help Dorothy return home to Kansas. When they enter the Wizard's presence, they discover that he's quite different than they had expected. Dorothy and her friends are confronted by an enormous floating green head that bellows with a terrifying voice, amid puffs of smoke and shooting flames. Unafraid, Dorothy's little dog, Toto, runs to the side of the room and pulls back a curtain. To everyone's amazement, the great Wizard of Oz is nothing more than an absent-minded little man maneuvering levers and amplifying his voice. The Great Wizard is all smoke and mirrors.

Sometimes we are too. Our shame can only be healed when we pull back the curtain and allow ourselves to be seen for who we really are.

### Overcome the Enemy's Lies with the Voice of Love

Next, we overcome our shame by identifying the core beliefs and convictions that contradict God's truth about who we are. But identifying the shame is only the starting point. Insight alone cannot change the human heart. Real change requires something more. In the battle against shame, we must counter its voices with the voice of Love—the voice of God, revealed in the person of Jesus. I'll explain this later.

As we begin to identify and accept this voice, however, we also encounter static from the voices of our past. One of the Enemy's most cunning forms of deception is to coax us into beating ourselves up, making ourselves pay, rejecting our true identities—in effect, hating ourselves. Henri Nouwen knew from personal experience that self-loathing is a barrier to breaking free from shame: "Self-rejection is the greatest enemy of the spiritual life because it contradicts the sacred voice that calls us the 'Beloved.' Being the Beloved expresses the core truth of our existence."[5]

### Practice True Humility

The next leg of the journey in overcoming shame is learning to practice true humility. Notice that I said *true* humility, because humility is often misunderstood as a subtle form of shaming and self-rejection—feeling so bad about yourself that you won't repeat whatever offense you committed. But truly humble people do not feel self-contempt. Thomas Merton wrote that humility consists of being "precisely the person you actually are before God."[6] At the core of humility is trust—trusting God, and trusting others with who you are. This explains why humility, if properly understood, is the antidote to shame. When Adam and Eve hid, God sought them out and called, "Where are you?" The hopeful and beautiful truth is that God is calling out for you too.

## THE VOICE OF LOVE SPEAKS LOUDER THAN THE VOICE OF SHAME

Several years after my healing from sexual addiction, I began another leg in my journey toward wholeness that was totally unexpected. I began experiencing random flashbacks that left me traumatized.

A psychologist eventually diagnosed me with post-traumatic stress disorder resulting from my childhood sexual abuse. Many combat veterans experience this disorder after coming home from battle. In severe cases, they may be walking down the street, hear a helicopter overhead, and suddenly, reflexively, start running for protection under a picnic table or in a Dumpster. Though living in the present, their emotions and physiological responses convince them that they are actually reliving the moment of trauma.

I discovered early in this journey that when the flashbacks occurred, my walk-in closet was one of the only places I felt physically and emotionally safe. One time, a very severe flashback thrust me back in my mind to the pain and violation that had been inflicted on me well over forty years before. As cortisol, adrenaline, and other brain chemicals surged through my bloodstream, my heart began to race, my chest grew tight, and the feelings of abuse washed over me all over again. Suddenly, I became that little boy, and all rational, adultlike thinking disappeared. I crawled to my closet and began weeping uncontrollably, curling up in a ball and wrapping myself in a quilt.

After twenty minutes or so, the flashback passed. Exhausted, I continued lying there in the darkness of my closet. I heard the doorbell ring downstairs, followed by the excited voices of my wife and kids. My friend Eric, a twenty-year police veteran and SWAT team hostage negotiator, was at the door. Because of our friendship, I was acutely aware that police officers are tough and rarely show any weakness. Hiding in my closet, I felt relieved knowing I wouldn't have to deal with him.

Just then, deep in my heart, I heard a voice. It was a voice of Love, the Voice of my heavenly Father. He spoke to me as I burrowed into the quilt, alone in the dark closet, with swollen eyes. *I want you to invite Eric into this closet with you. I want to show you My love through him,* said the Voice.

"But I'm almost naked, there's snot running down my face, and I can't stop crying," I answered.

*I want you to receive My love through him,* the Voice replied.

I knew this was the voice of God. But in my pride and fear, I resolved that there was no way I would allow Eric into that closet to see me in this shameful condition. Just then, Julianne knocked on the door to check on me. I'll never forget what happened next. As she opened the door, I knew that my greatest desire—to be loved and accepted for who I really was—was deeper and truer than my fear of being rejected. So I said to my wife, "Honey, please get Eric. I want him to see me."

Moments later my friend stood in the doorway of the closet. As he slowly knelt down and rested his hand on me to comfort me, I had never felt so vulnerable, exposed, and naked. I was surprised, however, because I also had never felt so deeply loved and known. In that moment I knew I had nothing to hide, nothing to lose, and nothing to prove. It was a completely new experience of freedom. By humbling myself and inviting Eric into my shame, I opened my heart to receive the love of Christ through the presence of my friend. In that series of eternal moments, he became the hands and feet of Jesus. The voice of Love began countering my lifelong voices of shame.

All of us have hiding places where we stow away our shame. Where do you hide yours? What memories or triggers send you scurrying for cover? If the voice of shame could be silenced, what do you think the voice of Love might say to you? What do you long to hear? Who might be an Eric to you—someone you could invite into your shame who would not be frightened by your nakedness? Who can you trust with *you*?

7

# The Soul Snare Path

The question for our lives is not whether we will
surrender, but to whom or what we will surrender.
**—GORDON DALBEY, *FIGHT LIKE A MAN*[1]**

"If I don't jump in right away, I may not share what I want to,"
Aidan asserted. "I know I'm here for spiritual direction before my
sabbatical, but I think I need to start with a time of confession."

After enduring two years of soul-crushing church conflict
that led to a church division, Aidan's leadership team provided
him with a much-needed six-month sabbatical. At the outset of
his time away, he came to Colorado to participate in a two-week
soul care intensive with Restoring the Soul, the ministry where
I serve.

I begin every intensive, regardless of the presenting issue, by
giving every person or couple a DVD titled *Somebody's Daughter:
A Journey to Freedom from Pornography. Somebody's Daughter* is
an intense documentary that includes interviews with a pastor, a
businessman, a couple, and me as we share about the destructive
effects of porn on our lives. That night Aidan watched the DVD
in his hotel room. He was so deeply convicted that he hadn't slept
most of the night.

Aidan's unplanned confession that day exposed an on-again,

off-again struggle with porn since he was sixteen. When the conflict in his church heated up, his struggle was on again with an increased intensity that terrified him. Over the next nine days he spent three hours with me every morning, sharing his life story and his heart. We explored his hopes and dreams, as well as his brokenness and pain.

At the end of the two hard but fruitful weeks, Aidan remarked, "As I leave here today, I don't feel like it's the end, but a new beginning." Pulling back the curtain of secrecy and self-reliance allowed him to do some significant work. But he was right—it was only the beginning. His story clearly illustrates what I call the "soul snare cycle."

## IDENTIFYING YOUR SOUL SNARE CYCLE

Early in the Old Testament story, God's children begin a heartbreaking but predictable pattern. God calls them to give Him their hearts, they eventually give their hearts to other gods, God calls them back to Himself, they repent and humble themselves, they give their hearts to other gods, and so it goes. It sounds a lot like "lather, rinse, repeat," doesn't it?

With my own sexual addiction history, as well as every man's with whom I've worked, a similar cycle plays out. Being able to identify our soul snare cycle can help us in at least three ways. First, it gives us a sense that our feelings, behavior, and thought patterns are not random and completely unpredictable. Knowing the pattern and issues contributing to the obsession is empowering.

Second, understanding the cycle as it applies to our individual stories allows us to identify what is happening beneath the surface in our souls. Linking the pattern of porn use to our brokenness and emotions allows us to see what drives our behavior. As we realize what drives our behavior, our areas of brokenness are exposed, and deep healing can begin.

Third, once we identify the pattern and our reasons for acting out, we can understand why the soul snare cycle is a vicious never ending sequence, as illustrated below.

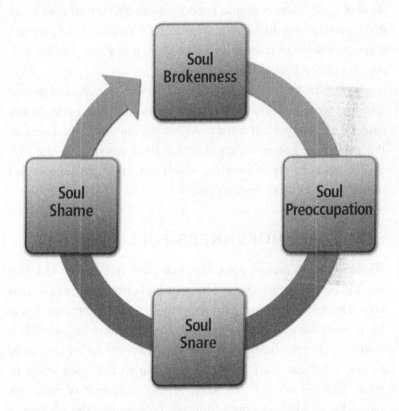

The soul snare cycle begins with our *soul brokenness*—wickedness, woundedness, weakness, and warfare. These are the logs and branches vulnerable to being ignited. The next stage of the cycle involves our triggers—people, places, events, and experiences that light the kindling of our brokenness on fire and set the cycle in motion. The cycle then leads us to *soul preoccupation*, when our focus, attention, and passion become absorbed and directed toward the pursuit of sexual gratification. After that, we enter the *soul snare* by crossing the line from desire to action, anticipation, and indulgence. The soul snare cycle then leads us to the *soul shame* stage. Not only do we feel a great sense of regret, guilt, or shame, but our actions also confirm our belief in our personal worthlessness and inadequacy. Finally, in the penance stage, we resolve to change our behavior in a way that actually perpetuates the cycle of addiction.

Each time the cycle concludes and repeats, we descend deeper into a downward spiral that reinforces the previous cycle. In my case, I turned to porn and sex to relieve the pain of my brokenness. But each time I gave in, my shame poured gasoline on the fire, which increased my brokenness, which in turn increased my need to find relief. Lather, rinse, repeat.

## HOW OUR BROKENNESS FUELS THE FIRE

We know we're broken men. But how does our brokenness play out in the soul snare cycle? The soul brokenness stage primarily concerns itself with our pain, emptiness, and discontent. These feelings set the stage for the cyclical drama about to unfold. When feelings stemming from our brokenness arise, our reflex is to avoid or control them. Carl Jung was referring to this idea when he wrote that all neurosis is caused by the avoidance of necessary pain.[2] By avoiding or controlling our brokenness, the whisper of porn becomes a shout, and the lying promises of porn begin to sound like a sensible solution. We profoundly mishandle the ache of living in a fallen world.

At any given time, our brokenness is never far away. We may appear together or relatively whole, but beneath the surface things are usually not as they seem. We all carry pain and unfinished business from our pasts.

As we explored his story, Aidan discovered that the combination of his father's control and perfectionism had wounded his soul deeply. In the attempt to measure up to his father's expectations, he earned a doctorate in theology and entered pastoral ministry. But his polished exterior couldn't change his core beliefs that he wasn't good enough and never would be. Ministry success became his anesthetic of choice for numbing the pain of never measuring up to his father's expectations. It gave him a false sense of affirmation and approval. So when things went south with his church, his inner self felt deflated and without an identity. That's when he returned to porn.

Along with the pain of our pasts, we all feel pain and discontent in the present. Many of us resemble the proverbial frog in the pot. Drop the frog into the boiling water, and it jumps out. Drop it into a pot of cold water, heat it slowly, and it never perceives the danger. We, too, can be oblivious to the danger of living with an ever-increasing accumulation of stress or conflict—until the temperature of life puts us in danger.

For most of his life, Aidan suspected that the unresolved issues with his father prevented his heart from being free. But he wasn't prepared for the day-to-day pain, contention, and turmoil he experienced during the two-year church conflict. He was diagnosed with skin cancer, his wife was diagnosed with breast cancer requiring a double mastectomy, and he was engaged in ongoing litigation with the builder of his home due to some faulty engineering. On the outside he appeared to be weathering the storm, grateful for a close few who prayed for his strength and perseverance. On the inside he questioned God, fantasized about getting out of ministry, and became increasingly resentful of other people's needs. His soul was thirsty for God but was absorbed by porn.

## WHAT TRIGGERS YOUR LUST?

Triggers are feelings, people, places, circumstances, or events that you associate with your lust and porn use. Like a doctor tapping your knee with a rubber mallet and your leg reflexively extending outward, triggers are cues that reflexively elicit cravings and desire for porn. *External triggers* can be obvious—like getting an e-mail solicitation for porn or seeing a beer commercial where an attractive woman bends over a pool table. External triggers may also be less obvious, like being home alone, having unrestricted computer access, or interacting with someone you find sexually attractive.

*Internal triggers* include feelings and thoughts. Emotions such as disappointment, loneliness, rejection, anxiety, anger, and boredom are common triggers. Physical feelings, including fatigue, headaches, hunger, or chronic pain, can also serve as internal triggers. Thoughts can be more subtle internal triggers. A few examples include: *I've been working so hard I deserve to reward myself . . . My girlfriend is so inattentive . . . My boss never appreciates me . . . If I were a real man, I'd know how to rock climb (or fix my own brakes).*

Triggers are unique to each man; however, every man who has been triggered will experience two separate reactions. First, his trigger causes a very real and very powerful physiological reaction in the body. The moment a man is triggered, dopamine—a powerful chemical known as the "gotta have it" molecule—is released in the brain. The more often this chemical reaction occurs, the more the trigger is reinforced. As a result, it becomes more and more difficult to "just say no." More on this in chapter 10.

Once the trigger is tripped, a second common reaction begins as an inner dialogue takes place. The trigger proposes a solution to the problem of your underlying brokenness. Following are some common scenarios Aidan encountered that describe how triggers provide a solution to the problem.

| | | |
|---|---|---|
| **Our brokenness** | → | I feel overwhelmed with my life, I'm tired, and I have no energy to get things done today. |
| **The trigger's solution** | → | Porn will relieve my stress, increase my energy, and give me something to focus on. |
| **Our brokenness** | → | No woman would want me if she really knew me. I don't have what it takes to win a woman. |
| **The trigger's solution** | → | Porn "wants" me. With porn I do have what it takes. |
| **Our brokenness** | → | I feel powerless with my wife, who always wins. |
| **The trigger's solution.** | → | Porn will make me feel powerful. I'll show her. |

At first, Aidan didn't realize he was being triggered. Over time he began to identify the triggers that were unique to him. As he did, the power of the soul snare cycle became even clearer.

## WHY ARE WE SO PREOCCUPIED?

Once triggered, porn pulls us into its gravitational vortex. This is the preoccupation stage. Once a man reaches this, without some major interruption or intervention, he will very likely act out. Three phases comprise the preoccupation stage. Phase one occurs as *passion is awakened*. If being triggered is like jerking the pull cord of a lawn mower to start the engine, then the preoccupation stage propels the lawn mower forward. A man may feel sexually aroused, but more often than not, what he first experiences is a mood lift, a boost of energy, or wind in the sails of his soul.

Although I have not acted out sexually since 1994, at times the battle with lust can be intense. Recently, I noticed a pattern I had not been aware of. Whenever I would go to the grocery store, I made it a point to walk down the magazine aisle. As I walked past glossy covers featuring celebrities and models, I discovered that my energy and mood lifted ever so slightly. Even though I wasn't stopping to focus on any given magazine, just walking past those images was like an afternoon shot of espresso.

The moment we become preoccupied, our brains start releasing dopamine and adrenaline, our energy levels may increase, and our deflated souls begin to fill and rise like a balloon inflated with helium. I know men who haven't looked at porn in years but who virtually live in the preoccupation stage. Their minds are constantly on the prowl for sexual stimulation, and they justify it because they aren't using porn.

Phase two occurs when *attention is focused*. Borrowing from the movie *Top Gun*, I call this "radar lock." Just as a fighter jet locks on its enemy target, passion and desire lock on and lock into porn. Dopamine—the "gotta have it" molecule—which the brain releases during the trigger stage, begins to increase, rendering a man more and more absorbed. One man described it this way: "It's like I'm standing in the desert, and suddenly I see an oasis. All I can think about and all I'm aware of is getting to that oasis. I may be in the middle of a meeting at work, or talking to my wife, but I'm no longer really there—I'm off to the oasis."

As men, we also need to be aware of the level of our preoccupation with porn. Some men may only seek out porn once a month, while others find themselves spiraling out of control multiple times per day. Prior to the painful church conflict, Aidan acted out once or twice a year. Despite his ongoing, underlying issues, he was able to "manage" his sin. But the addition of the church conflict to his health and family issues became too much, and his porn struggle escalated. When he finally shared with me about his struggle, he was spending upwards of three hours per day online.

The final phase in the preoccupation cycle is when *arrangements are made*. At this point a man begins to lay the groundwork for how he will act out with porn. He may be driving to a business meeting and planning to check out some porn on his smartphone. He may spend the morning fantasizing while working at his desk, as he anticipates masturbating in the men's room at lunch. He may offer to "work on the bills" on Saturday morning while his wife runs the kids to gymnastics—when he is actually planning to surf for porn. Of course, some men are triggered, become preoccupied, and act out immediately. Every man has his own path that ensnares him.

## HOW OUR SOULS BECOME ENSNARED

Though you won't find "addiction" when you search for it in your Bible software program, Scripture clearly teaches that we can become enslaved to ungodly passions (Rom. 6:19; Titus 3:3). To be enslaved means that we are captive and no longer free, powerless to emancipate ourselves. This is why Paul cried out, "Who will rescue me?" (Rom. 7:24). One of the most striking images in Scripture describes the reality of addictive passions as a snare. The writer of Proverbs tells us that "in the paths of the wicked lie thorns and snares, but he who guards his soul stays far from them" (22:5).

Many modern-day readers may not be familiar with a snare. For millennia, hunters have used snares—nooses made of rope or wire— to trap their prey. To attract the object of their desire, they place a lure, usually a delectable piece of meat, within the snare's loop. In the attempt to consume the bait, the animal steps into the snare and sets it off. The harder the victim tries to break free from the snare, the tighter it becomes. The Old Testament relates that we can be ensnared by our own sinful choices (Prov. 29:6) and by our worship of idols or other gods (Ex. 23:33; Deut. 7:16).

One especially pernicious way of becoming ensnared is through sexual sin. When Solomon offered his counsel to men regarding the allure and danger of sexual sin, he used the imagery of a deer stepping into a noose and a bird darting into a snare (Prov. 7:1–23). The writer of Ecclesiastes warned of the woman whose "heart is a trap and whose hands are chains." Then he concluded, "The man who pleases God will escape her, but the sinner she will ensnare" (7:26).

### The Surrender Principle

As a person becomes ensnared by something like porn, two different dynamics take place. I call the first one the *surrender principle*. Simply put, our hearts attach to anything to which they have surrendered. We can surrender our hearts in ways that are beautiful. Many people describe their conversion experiences as "giving my heart to Christ." Or on a wedding day, we may speak of "giving my heart" to our beloved. Surrendering our hearts in this way can be life-giving as we become more of who God designed us to be.

We can also surrender our hearts in ways that diminish us. For example, we can surrender them to a substance, like food; an action or activity, like sex or gambling or shopping; or a person, such as a spouse, a romantic interest, even a child. Paul knew that when we surrender who we are, we are no longer free.

> Do not offer the parts of your body to sin, as instruments of wickedness. (Rom. 6:13)

> Don't you realize that you become the slave of whatever you choose to obey? (Rom. 6:16 NLT)

Paul knew that when we surrender our hearts to something, our hearts attach to it.

### The Attachment Principle

The second dynamic that takes place when we become ensnared is what I call the *attachment principle*. This occurs after we have yielded our hearts to some thing, person, or process. When we attach, we are no longer free. Gerald May has written: "In the great spiritual traditions of the world, attachments are seen as any concerns that usurp our desire for love, anything that becomes more important to us than God. Paul Tillich said that whatever we are ultimately concerned with is God for us. At any given moment, that with which we are most concerned is most likely to be something other than the true God."[3]

So the man whose heart is surrendered to porn will become attached to porn. The more frequently he surrenders, the stronger the attachment becomes. The porn and lust that initially appeared to be serving him have now become his master. He is bound and compelled. He is ensnared.

## OUR SHAME FUELS OUR BROKENNESS

In the soul snare cycle, the shame stage is most insidious. Many men experience significant healing of their brokenness, only to remain caught in the snare. This usually takes place because the tentacles of shame still hold these men tightly in their grip. At this point in the cycle, two kinds of shame must be addressed. The first kind results from the compulsive acts themselves. *I can't believe what I've done*, a man may think.

The second kind of shame results from the core beliefs that have been present in the man all along. *I'm basically a bad [or worthless] person. I'm not good enough. I don't measure up. Nobody would love me as I am. I can't get my needs met by depending on others.*

The subtlest consequence of advancing this far in the cycle is that our shame is layered on top of our brokenness. In other words, our shame fuels brokenness *and* our shame adds to brokenness. The cycle is vicious. A man thinks to himself, *If I felt bad about myself before I indulged in porn, now I really have reason to feel bad.* The shame stage must be struck a deathblow. Though it's hard to believe at the start, when a man begins to deal with his shame, the compulsion toward porn often significantly lessens.

## PENANCE AND THE HEART'S CRY FOR FREEDOM

The penance stage is closely related to the shame stage because through it we respond to shame. In the penance stage a man takes the shame he carries and attempts to overcome it somehow through performance. It's an unconscious way of atoning for our sin, because deep down we believe our struggle makes us less acceptable to God. Most of the time we act out our penance subconsciously. Stories from men in the penance stage can be heartbreaking. I've known men who physically harm their genitals to punish themselves. Some men have fasted from food after acting out sexually, presumably to regain control of their appetite or to express remorse. I've known men who act out their penance by bringing their wives or girlfriends flowers or by being extra attentive. When my porn struggle was at its worst, I harmfully pushed my body beyond its limits. A number of times, I ran around the local track until I made myself sick or exercised to the point of exhaustion. My most common form of penance, however, was bittersweet—I memorized large passages of Scripture. Though today I admit that it has served me well, at the time I did it because I believed I was unacceptable to God just the way I was.

Despite the presence of our addictions and compulsions with

porn, deep within, our hearts cry for freedom. The soul snare cycle is a description of the pattern of enslavement. But there's good news. You can walk a path that leads to freedom, which we'll explore just ahead.

John Donne was a sixteenth-century poet, philosopher, and priest. At some point in his life, he was renowned for spending large sums of money on womanizing, hobbies, and travel. Knowing that God alone was the source of salvation from his compulsions, he penned these words of surrender to God from his Holy Sonnet 14:

> Batter my heart, three-person'd God; for you
> As yet but knock; breathe, shine, and seek to mend;
> That I may rise, and stand, o'erthrow me, and bend
> Your force, to break, blow, burn, and make me new.
> I, like an usurp'd town, to another due,
> Labour to admit you, but O, to no end.
> Reason, your viceroy in me, me should defend,
> But is captived, and proves weak or untrue.
> Yet dearly I love you, and would be loved fain,
> But am betroth'd unto your enemy;
> Divorce me, untie, or break that knot again,
> Take me to you, imprison me, for I,
> Except you enthrall me, never shall be free,
> Nor ever chaste, except you ravish me.[4]

". . . for I, except you enthrall me, never shall be free." This is the ultimate goal of turning from being enthralled with porn. Our hearts are freed from the fixation on porn to be captivated by the beauty of God's love, all so that our hearts can be given more fully to God and others. In the chapter ahead we will discuss how God has actually taken initiative toward making this happen.

8

# Your Good Heart

The freedom question, then, is not whether
we can do whatever we want, but whether
we can do what we most deeply want.

**—GERALD MAY, *THE AWAKENED HEART***[1]

What do you want?

**—JESUS OF NAZARETH (JOHN 1:38)**

"Can we spend some time together, Larry?" I asked. "I'm struggling with sexual temptation, and I'd like to talk with you about it."

While serving a postgraduate internship with author and psychologist Larry Crabb, I had finally summoned the courage to ask for help. Fortunately, he said yes. Unfortunately, I applied the "97% rule," which states that when sharing with a fellow Christian about your sexual sin, make sure you never share the most intimate 3 percent. Despite my outright deception, our conversation planted seeds in my heart that could not bear fruit until they were buried in the ground and died.

"I'm really, really, struggling with lust and wanting to look at pornography," I admitted. By then I had done a whole lot more than that, but being transparent was a big deal for me. Larry could see I was torn over my struggle, so he asked me some probing questions about my life story and sexual history.

At the end of our conversation, he caught me totally off guard. "If what you *really* want to do is look at porn," he said, "then go ahead and look at porn."

"Yeah, right. Like I'm really going to do that." I chuckled cynically.

Larry just looked at me, dead serious, and repeated himself. "If what you *really* want to do is look at porn and masturbate, then go ahead and do it." I could tell he wasn't being flippant, but I also knew his integrity.

So I launched back at him, "I know this must be some kind of reverse psychology or paradoxical treatment you're trying on me, right?" The look on his face, however, told me this was not his intention.

"I don't get it," I exclaimed. "Why are you telling me to go ahead and look at porn and masturbate?" In frustration, I hit my fist against the armchair and shouted, "That's not what I want to do!"

Larry's eyes sparkled with delight. "Exactly!" he cheered. "That's the point. Looking at pornography and masturbating is *not what you really want to do.*"

I was speechless. *Could it really be true? Despite my out-of-control passions, could a passion for God inside me run deeper than my desire for sex and porn?* For the first time in my life, I felt truly hopeful that my heart was not defined by lust. That something good, noble, and godly dwelled within me that was not based upon my performance, faithfulness, or even resistance to temptation.

I discovered that day what Scripture describes as my new heart. But before taking a deeper look at our new, good hearts we first must understand our old hearts, the hearts that have not yet been made new through Christ.

## THE REASON FOR THE GOSPEL—
## OUR HEARTS ARE BENT AWAY FROM GOD

Our hearts haven't always tilted away from God. Our story didn't begin with sin. God created man and woman in His image, and bestowed upon them glory, beauty, and dignity, which still reside deep within us today. However, when our ancestors in the garden of Eden ate the fruit that God commanded them not to eat, they took matters into their own hands and chose self-sufficiency over trusting in their Creator. The writer of Ecclesiastes put it this way: "This only have I found: God made mankind upright, but men have gone in search of many schemes" (7:29). This is the essence of sin and the proclivity of every human being without Christ. We are bent in a direction away from God.

As the story of humanity unfolds, this bent plays out dramatically. The first murder occurred when Adam and Eve's son Cain killed his brother, Abel. And as people began to multiply and fill the earth, God was grieved by humanity's increasing wickedness. Within a few generations we read that "the LORD saw how great man's wickedness on the earth had become, and that every inclination of the thoughts of his heart was only evil all the time" (Gen. 6:5).

So God initiated another rescue plan. He destroyed nearly all of creation in a flood and started over with Noah and his family. When Noah stepped out of the ark, he built an altar to God, and God in turn entered into a covenant with Noah and his descendants. God promised to never again destroy all living things. He then blessed Noah's family and commanded them to be fruitful and multiply.

But things didn't turn out much better this time either, as people continued to turn their backs on Him. Once again He initiated a plan to save them by making a covenant with Abraham. He promised that all the peoples of the earth would be blessed through him (Gen. 12:3). Within a few generations Abraham's descendants ended up in slavery in Egypt and forgot about their God. Yet once again God rescued them. He delivered them from Egypt and entered into a covenant with them through Moses, who gave them God's law on stone tablets.

Do you see a pattern here? Throughout Scripture, God initiated a number of covenants, or formal agreements, with His people. They weren't legal documents, like a mortgage closing; they were covenants of God's promise of rescue. In the Old Testament, the best word to describe a covenant is *salvation*. God initiated a way to save and set apart a people whom He could call His own.

But sin and wickedness had unleashed a domino chain of unbelief, idolatry, and self-centeredness, resulting in a world that was a far cry from Eden. So God sent prophets to call His people to repentance. The prophet Jeremiah summed up the pattern of God's people this way: "The heart is deceitful above all things, and desperately wicked" (Jer. 17:9 KJV).

The pattern of our bent away from God prompted a repeated declaration: "There is no one righteous, not even one; there is no one who understands, no one who seeks God" (Rom. 3:10–11; see also Pss. 14:1–3; 53:1–3; Eccl. 7:20).

Without a substantial change in the very core of the human heart, the pattern of wickedness would play out again and again for eternity. God needed to address the problem of human sin on the deepest possible level. So He set a plan in motion that He had determined before the foundations of the world, a plan that would reach to the very core of who men and women would become in Christ.

## WE NEEDED A HEART TRANSPLANT

Some years ago a man said to me, "I wish I could go to a hospital and have my sexual addiction surgically removed!" Although he spoke in jest, his desire for healing was intense, and he knew he needed to get to the heart of his problem. Wouldn't it be nice if a doctor could give us an anesthetic and then extract our sinful patterns—just like a ruptured spleen or an inflamed appendix? Of course, no such operation for the soul exists. And if it did, it still wouldn't deal with the problem.

In the Sermon on the Mount, Jesus addressed the issue of lust: "I tell you that anyone who looks at a woman lustfully has already committed adultery with her in his heart" (Matt. 5:28). Most of us have heard and felt the weight of these words. But what Jesus said next put His famous teaching about lust in a crucial context: "If your right eye causes you to sin, gouge it out and throw it away. It is better for you to lose one part of your body than for your whole body to be thrown into hell. And if your right hand causes you to sin, cut it off and throw it away. It is better for you to lose one part of your body than for your whole body to go into hell" (vv. 29–30).

These seem like bizarre words. Was Jesus advocating self-mutilation? No. Perhaps Jesus was asking us to be radical—do whatever it takes to avoid sin. Take drastic measures. If your computer is causing you to sin, get rid of it, and so on. Of course, we ought to resist sin, but this explanation misses the point entirely.

In the Sermon on the Mount Jesus turned the teaching of the religious leaders upside down. What constitutes murder? Being angry or calling someone a fool (Matt. 5:21–22). So, will putting duct tape over someone's mouth change this? No, it's an issue of the heart. What defines adultery? Just looking at a woman lustfully (Matt. 5:27–28). So, will gouging out your eye change this? No, it's a heart issue.

Throughout the rest of the sermon, Jesus made the point that obedience to the law begins and ends with the heart. Let's face it: a blind person is just as capable of lusting as you and I are. Physical surgery won't cure our lust. Jesus knew better than anyone else that the surgical procedure we needed was a heart transplant, not dismemberment.

## THE REST OF THE GOSPEL— HEARTS BENT TOWARD GOD

Dallas Willard has suggested that much of what passes for the gospel today is a reduced gospel, a gospel that simply involves believing the right things and being forgiven.[2] This has led to a kind of Christianity focused on life *then* and not life *now*, where spiritual maturity is defined by what our lives look like on the outside.

The gospel—the good news—is truly extraordinary news because it doesn't concern itself with just getting to heaven. It concerns itself with life *now*. We rarely hear preachers say that in addition to forgiveness and assurance of salvation, something crucial has been restored to us. God has worked in such a way that our hearts that were bent *away* from God (before Christ) are now bent *toward* God because of Christ.

The same prophets who spoke of the depths of wickedness in the hearts of men also foretold of God's ultimate resolution to the deep issue of sin in our hearts. A plan so radical that it would cost God everything:

> *He was pierced for our transgressions,*
> *he was crushed for our iniquities;*
> *the punishment that brought us peace was upon him,*
> *and by his wounds we are healed.*
> *We all, like sheep, have gone astray,*
> *each of us has turned to his own way;*
> *and the LORD has laid on him*
> *the iniquity of us all. (Isa. 53:5–6)*

By sending Jesus, God brought His rescue effort to a whole new level. Instead of dealing with sin the same old way, with a system of sacrificing lambs and other animals, God Himself provided the lamb—the Lamb of God, Jesus. As a result, our sins were washed away (1 Cor. 6:11), and God has removed our sins as far as the east is from the west (Ps. 103:12).

In Jesus, God ushered in a new covenant. Remember what Jesus said at the Last Supper? "This cup is the new covenant in my blood, which is poured out for you" (Luke 22:20). What He meant was that, through Him, God faithfully brought salvation, just as He did before. But this time He offered a radical operation that dealt with sin at the deepest possible level—our hearts.

> "This is the covenant I will make with the house of Israel
>     after that time," declares the LORD.
> "I will put my law in their minds
>     and write it on their hearts.
> I will be their God,
>     and they will be my people." (Jer. 31:33)

Previously God's laws were written on stone tablets; now God would write them in our hearts and minds. The law had existed outside of us; now it would reside inside of us.

Ezekiel also spoke of the promised new covenant with even more detail. His description went even further than the other Old Testament prophets': "I will sprinkle clean water on you, and you will be clean; I will cleanse you from all your impurities and from all your idols. I will give you a new heart and put a new spirit in you; I will remove from you your heart of stone and give you a heart of flesh. And I will put my Spirit in you and move you to follow my decrees and be careful to keep my laws" (36:25–27).

God revealed that He would make us utterly clean and pure.

It would require exchanging our old hearts and identities for new ones. Our hearts of stone would be replaced by hearts of flesh. Finally, by putting His Spirit within us, we would be empowered to obey. We would obey Him not because we had to, but because we *wanted* to.

The New Testament describes Jesus as the mediator of the new covenant (Heb. 12:24), because God placed His law—Jesus, the fulfillment of the law—within our hearts. Instead of writing His law on tablets of stone, He has written it on tablets of the human heart.

I can't think of any more pertinent theological truth or exciting promise for hope to share with the man trapped in sexual compulsion than the idea of the new covenant. The truth is this: God has dealt with sin in your heart. And having a new heart changes everything—including what you do with your eyes and hands and other body parts.

## YOUR GOOD HEART IS WHAT IS MOST TRUE ABOUT YOU

When I placed my faith in Christ at the age of sixteen, I did so for two reasons. I needed forgiveness, and I wanted to go to heaven. From the teaching I had heard, through Jesus' death on the cross, my relationship with God was restored and the debt for my sins was paid. As a result, I was forgiven, and I was assured of going to heaven. Little did I know that although these truths were certainly real, the gospel involved so much more. I had no idea that my heart had been made new or what that actually meant. I had no idea that salvation was an absolutely essential door I entered, so that in Christ I might experience restoration.

When you place your faith in Christ, something substantively changes inside of you. Various terms in Scripture describe this transformation. Jesus called it being "born again" (John 3:3). Paul referred to it as regeneration, or "renewal by the Holy Spirit" (Titus 3:5). In reality, the substantive change that has occurred is a heart transplant.

In conversation after conversation, men tell me that the reason they struggle with lust and porn is because their "heart is . . . desperately wicked," referring to Jeremiah 17:9 (KJV). But for the man who has trusted Christ, this is a paralyzing mistake. God has given him *a new heart.* His heart is no longer desperately wicked. This is no small theological side issue.

What *is* true, if you belong to God, is that you have a good heart. In the *deepest part* of who you are, you have a passion to love God and walk in His ways. This statement isn't based on mere emotion. It is a present reality. At this very moment, regardless of whether you looked at porn this morning or masturbated last night, God says this about you and to you:

- You are pure and clean (1 John 1:5–9).
- You are without stain or blemish (Eph. 5:27).
- You are the righteousness of God (2 Cor. 5:21).
- Christ lives in you (Gal. 2:20).
- Your heart is alive to God (Rom. 6:11).
- You are a new man (2 Cor. 5:17).
- You have a good and noble heart (Luke 8:15).

Your sin nature is not your true identity. It's not your deepest nature and it's no longer your controlling disposition, proclivity, or propensity. Sin no longer defines you. Instead, here is the deepest truth about you: your sinful nature has been put off, or stripped away (Col. 2:11), and you are dead to your sinful nature (Rom. 6:11).

Make no mistake. Your sin nature, or your flesh, is alive and well. Your lust for porn, your objectification of women, your demand to have your desires gratified—they are proof enough of it. But your flesh—your sin nature—*no longer forms the core of your identity.* Your sinful nature is no longer who you are.

## WHEN WHAT YOU WANT IS NOT WHAT YOU REALLY WANT

Right now you might be thinking, *That's all well and good, and that all might even be true. But why do I still feel controlled by lust and porn?*

Remember the cry of Paul's heart in Romans 7, which we explored back in chapter 1? Even he struggled with sins that he didn't want to commit. But he made it abundantly clear: "*It is no longer I myself who do it,* but it is sin living in me. I know that nothing good lives in me, that is, *in my sinful nature*" (7:17–18, emphasis added). Was Paul passing the buck so he wouldn't have to take responsibility? Was he going light on sin? Absolutely not. Paul was making a crucial distinction between his sinful nature (his flesh) and his true self—his new heart. He went on: "Now if I do what I do not want to do, it is no longer I who do it, but it is sin living in me that does it" (v. 20).

This is so important that I need to say it again. Paul was telling us that we are not our sin nature. Countless followers of Jesus have lived under a crippling theology that defines them by their sinful nature and a desperately wicked heart. But we must not confuse our sinful nature with our new hearts. Our sin nature was crucified with Christ. Our new hearts are alive with the very life of God beating in us. And our new hearts are good hearts. Of course, we still need to resist sin and temptation, but we also need to know that something is energizing that sin. Beneath the sinful appetite resides a legitimate God-given desire springing from a God-given new heart.

When it seems all you want is the relief of an orgasm, something inside you wants more. When all you can think about is getting back to your hotel room so you can click on the adult pay-per-view, inside you desire something deeper. That is why Larry Crabb challenged me to press in to what I really wanted—what I was thirsty for. When all that compels you is the beauty of naked women, there is something more compelling within your heart. And you can learn to tap into that deeper desire.

## TURNING ON THE FLOW FROM THE SPRING WITHIN

If you set a bowl of carrot and celery sticks beside a bowl of potato chips on a table, which would seem more appealing and appetizing? I've always known that vegetables are good for me, and that chips may be an unhealthy option. But knowing that fact has rarely made a difference in my appetite. I want the chips! For the first twenty years of following Jesus, I associated God's ways with the carrots and celery, and my ways with the potato chips. I assumed that even though I knew His ways were better, my natural inclination gravitated toward lust and illicit sex.

The gospel turns all of this upside down. The reality of the new covenant and your new heart is that deep down, your inclination now gravitates toward God's heart and ways. "Delight yourselves in the LORD and he will give you the desires of your heart" (Ps. 37:4).

At my office I have two brass spigots that I purchased at a hardware store. One spigot has a red knob and represents how we often approach the Christian life. The assumption is that the source from which the water flows is a cesspool, so we focus our energies on turning the faucet off. The second spigot has a blue knob, and the assumption is that its source is a reservoir of good, clean water. Our goal with this spigot is to turn the faucet on—to release what is stored up. This spigot represents how we should live our lives in Christ, especially in regard to our recovery from porn.

Following Jesus is not about not sinning; it's about releasing His life from within. Like turning on the faucet. The goal is not to turn off the faucet of lust, but to turn on the faucet of trust. Trusting that God has restored my heart, and that my heart is good. Slowly, I began to understand just how much energy I had spent on sin management, trying to repress the cesspool I imagined within and keep the sewage inside from spewing out. As I stopped putting my energy into shutting off the faucet from the cesspool, my real passions began rising to the surface. The pipes in my soul were getting unclogged, and something was starting to flow that I didn't know was there. I began experiencing what Jesus described as "a spring of water welling up to eternal life" (John 4:14).

## WHAT DEFINES YOU?

Over the years I have led groups for men struggling with compulsive sexual behavior. At the start of each group, a different man takes his turn lighting a candle and recites something like this: "First, we light the candle to acknowledge the presence of Jesus—the Light of the World—who lives in us. Second, we light the candle to declare that we are not defined by our darkness, but defined by the light of Christ."

When our groups began, I had no idea how a small, symbolic act could be so powerful in reminding us what is true. At our final group meeting, the men usually shared that their most memorable experience was lighting the candle. The truth is that the light of Christ defines us.

Remember my story about the cathedral in chapter 1? Little did I know that only months later my double life would be found out. As I sat in that magnificent edifice, I wrote a poem about my heart. It was a poem about the me who was truly meant to fly, despite giving away my feathers to pornography and other sexual sin. The words I wrote that cold night were a kind of foreshadowing of the path I would walk the rest of my life.

*I've got a very hungry heart*
*For attention and affection*
*But I'm tasting bitter fruit*
*To whet my appetite*

*I'm gazing at an image*
*To heal my wounded life*
*She's a beauty not my own*
*Someone else's wife.*

*I've got a very thirsty soul*
*To live with wild abandon*
*But I'm drawing from a well*
*Won't ever satisfy*

*Still I'm fighting with my passions*
*And promise Him each time*
*But temptation just consumes me*
*Though I try with all my might*

*In a quest for love I'm wandering*
*And presume another sunrise*
*I exhume a life of ancient lies*
*And bury all my dreams*

*But lately I've been pondering*
*And seeing with my blind eyes*
*His light that I'm defined by*
*And it's brighter than it seems.*

Sitting in that cathedral, I began to realize that my desire for attention and affection was good. My longing for beauty was good. My thirst to live with freedom and wild abandon was good. The light and passion inside me was good. My heart was good. Of course it was—it was the heart of Jesus.

Take a moment and read the last two lines of the poem again, and this time, take it personally. "His light that *I'm* defined by / And it's brighter than it seems." Did you get that? *You* are defined by His light. See, if Jesus Christ lives in you, yes, you are forgiven and cleansed from sin. But far more than that, your sinful heart has been made new. You have been given a new identity and a new nature, *defined by Christ's light*. A passion resides deep inside you that is stronger than your passion for porn, relief, comfort, or revenge. It is a passion to love God and walk in His ways, just as Christ did. What might it mean for you to fan *that* flame?

**9**

# The Invisible Battle

*The story of your life is the story of a long and
brutal assault on your heart by the one who
knows what you could be and fears it.*

**—JOHN ELDREDGE**

"How much is it to get in?" I asked, trying to mask my nervousness.

"Four dollars," grunted the man behind the counter, without looking up.

"I left my wallet in the car," I replied. "I'll be right back."

My wallet was in my back pocket, but it contained only two dollars, which was all the money I had for the next seven days. I walked out the front door desperate, as if I only had half the money needed for a lifesaving kidney transplant.

Back at my car, I scrounged for change in the glove compartment and beneath the floor mats. With the help of a used McDonald's straw, I jimmied loose some coins stuck between the seats and eventually scraped together another dollar in change. I ran back inside, cleared my throat, and petitioned the clerk, who was now absorbed in a *USA Today*.

"Umm . . . I'm a little short of the four bucks. Is there any way you could cut me some slack and let me in?" The man looked up knowingly from behind the counter and waved me forward.

Self-consciously, I walked through the turnstile, past the parted heavy red velvet curtains, and into the inner sanctum of the XXX theater. For nearly an hour I sat in the dark, with a dozen or so men—all of us sitting alone.

Never before had I risked acting out in public. Porn had always served as my private indulgence, masturbating to fantasies, porn magazines, and occasional videotapes, but that isolation only intensified my longing for human contact. Driving to the porn theater that night, I secretly hoped I might actually stumble onto something or encounter someone who would fulfill that longing.

And stumble I did. Going to that theater opened a doorway to a whole new world. Near that movie house was a nighttime carnival of darkness I never knew existed. Nightclubs, strip clubs, bars, hotels, parties, prostitutes, drugs, and the like were available, all for the taking. Something deep inside cried, *I want this!* And something replied, *All of this is yours.* Over the next few days, I dove in headfirst, as my addiction escalated rapidly. Within three days I had hired my first prostitute.

## WE LIVE IN A WORLD AT WAR

In light of current world conditions, few people would disagree that we are at war. Just look at ongoing problems with terrorism and countless murders from the illegal drug trade. Add to that grim reality the atrocities of genocide, childhood sex slavery, and sex trafficking, and few would deny the reality of evil.

But speak of evil in the form of living, breathing personal entities—Satan and demons—and, well, that seems a little extreme to most people. Despite the visible evidence of evil, plenty of skeptics refuse to believe in a source behind that evil. And I can certainly understand. Even as a Christian, I haven't always believed in the influence of evil spirits or demons. Until twelve years ago I held a strong—though largely unexamined—position against the direct influence of the Enemy in our lives. What would people think of me? Would I come across as some religious nut? As a part-time seminary professor, I didn't want to appear intellectually unsophisticated.

I remained resolute in my beliefs until I encountered man after man in my office who struggled with all kinds of sexual brokenness. One man confessed that every time he looked at porn and masturbated, he immediately heard an accusing voice telling him he would never be free. Another man hated himself for feeling pleasure during episodes of sexual abuse from an older cousin. He vowed he would never feel sexual pleasure again. Yet another man acted out sexually in public restrooms with other men. Whenever he would decide to disclose his struggle to his wife, he developed intense urges to kill himself. And another man regularly woke up from nightmares in the middle of the night, sensing a palpable presence of evil hovering above him.

Skeptics might logically explain each of these examples as a psychological symptom. You might be surprised to know that I agree—any of these *could be* psychological symptoms. But my views changed as the result of a personal encounter with evil.

At the time, I was counseling a man I'll call Jim. When we first started meeting, our times together seemed fairly normal. But after several sessions I began to notice a disturbing pattern. Immediately after meeting with him, I experienced a heavy, oppressive darkness, along with visions of intense, violent sexual imagery. The first time it happened, I brushed it off as residue from our conversation. The second and third times, I dismissed it as my own lust. Finally one night, I was getting ready for bed, brushing my teeth. As I looked into the bathroom mirror, I saw the same violent sexual images, but this time they were standing right in front of me. A chill ran up my spine, and the hairs on the back of my neck stood at attention. Not exactly the relaxing bedtime ritual I was used to.

Within minutes I was on the phone with my friend John, who served as pastor of prayer and healing ministries at a local church. I nervously described these experiences, and without a hint of panic or drama, John said, "Michael, that's spiritual warfare. Let's pray." The next ten minutes changed my life. As John prayed, the cold chill lifted, the images disappeared, and I felt a profound sense of peace. What I had experienced disproved everything I believed about evil.

Over the next year, somewhat timidly, I began reading and studying about spiritual warfare. What I discovered absolutely blew me away. We live in a world at war. That war involves a battle waged against *you* and *me*. The prized possession of that battle, the purpose for fighting that battle, is control of the human heart. Little did I know that blow by blow I was losing, until finally I totally succumbed. The night back in my twenties when I had bargained my way into the porn theater, I unknowingly stepped through a doorway of darkness. I didn't realize that with each sinful choice I made, with every magazine, video, and act of sexual sin, a door opened that gave up more and more ground to the Enemy. I didn't consciously sell my soul or worship Satan in any of my addictions. However, I can absolutely tell you that something in me yielded, surrendered to darkness.

Evil is real, and it has a name: Satan—the adversary, deceiver, father of lies. After being thrown out of heaven for cosmic treason, Satan and his legion of fallen angels have had one goal: to defame God (Gen. 3:1–4). The Enemy comes only to steal, kill, and destroy (John 10:10). He wants to devour you and all God intended you to be and to accomplish (1 Peter 5:8). He exists to block you, in whatever way possible, from becoming the man of God you were created to be. He hates your soul, hates God in you, and hates how your life can make God known. If he can't kill your body, he'll try to kill your soul. And if he can't kill your soul, he'll try to convince you to cover it with shame and get you to hide (Gen. 3:1–10). Or, more subtly, he will try to convince you that you'll never change: "For our struggle is not against flesh and blood, but against the rulers, against the authorities, against the powers of this dark world and against the spiritual forces of evil in the heavenly realms" (Eph. 6:12).

## YOUR SEXUALITY IS A TARGET

Have you ever noticed that for some people sexuality can be an experience of intense pleasure and joy, while for others it can be an experience of intense shame and pain? From day one of Adam and Eve's union, God intended for sexuality to be a good gift. Yet for many, sexuality is anything but good; instead, it provokes feelings of betrayal and violation, shame and pain.

In the span of a few moments, a young life can be changed when an uncle fondles his nephew's genitals at a family reunion. Seeing two people having sex online can be both confusing and arousing for a young boy. What causes this? Why does sex create such brokenness? Philip Yancey explained the mysterious and sacramental nature of human sexuality.

> In one sense, we are never more Godlike than in the act of sex.
> We make ourselves vulnerable. We risk. We give and receive in
> a simultaneous act. We feel a primordial delight, entering into
> the other in communion. Quite literally we make one flesh out
> of two different persons, experiencing for a brief time a unity
> like no other. Two independent beings open their inmost selves
> and experience not a loss but a gain. In some way—"a profound
> mystery"—not even Paul dared explore—this most human act
> reveals something of the nature of reality, God's reality, in his
> relations with creation and perhaps within the Trinity itself.[1]

Yancey said that "we are never more Godlike than in the act of sex." Mind-blowing, isn't it? If we are never more Godlike than in the act of sex, should it come as any surprise that the evil one would make the destruction and desecration of sex a primary target in his war against all that is good and glorious? This is so much bigger than being accountable to someone and trying to remain pure.

Theologian Christopher West remarked, "If the body and sex are meant to proclaim our union with God, and if there is an enemy who wants to separate us from God, what do you think he is going to attack? If we want to know what is most sacred in this world, all we need do is look at what is most violently profaned."[2]

Your sexuality is an intense battle because it is *the* arena where God desires to demonstrate who He is and what He's like. Through sexual intercourse, God desires to demonstrate what communion with Him is meant to be. It's the taste of the intimacy we crave. Let's take a look at just how the Enemy attempts to make this happen.

## SCHEMES OF THE ENEMY

Soldiers begin their training in boot camp for all the standard forms of combat. But once they arrive in a particular war zone, they urgently need to learn how the enemy fights. So they are given specific training in how to fight against invisible insurgents, potentially hostile civilians, and a radically different culture. They're educated about tactics such as suicide bombings and improvised explosive devices. In the same way, we must be aware of how *our* enemy operates. Paul encouraged us not to allow Satan to outwit us or be unaware of his schemes (2 Cor. 2:11).

In chapter 5 I explained how Satan tempted Jesus by appealing to three counterfeits: counterfeit good, counterfeit truth, and counterfeit worship. However, just after Satan tempted Jesus to turn stones into bread, he sneaked in a far subtler—and far more insidious—attack that every man needs to understand: "The devil led him to Jerusalem and had him stand on the highest point of the temple. 'If you are the Son of God,' he said, 'throw yourself down from here'" (Luke 4:9–10).

Do you see it? The devil didn't attempt a frontal attack; he tried to ambush Jesus from the flank. "*If* you are the son of God . . ." he said. Satan was talking trash to Jesus! It's like saying to Michael Jordan, "*If* you know how to play basketball . . ." Or closer to home, "*If* you were a real man . . ." But Jesus was unshakably solid in His identity. He neither caved in from insecurity nor acted out in self-defense. He knew who He was—the beloved Son of God—and He stood firm in that truth.

How many men have gotten caught in the snare of sexual compulsion because they had something to prove? Or because their identities were at stake? Do you recall "The Broken Promises of Porn" from chapter 2? Porn promises strength, power, and intimacy without needing to live out of a true heart. When your identity as a man is at stake, porn, power, or possessions will hold an irresistible appeal. What tempts you? What does that say about who you are? What is your true identity? Who are you really? What defines you? The car you drive? The clothes you wear? The Omega watch?

## IDOLS INVITE DEMONIC ATTACHMENTS

In 1 Corinthians 10:20 Paul explained that demons are attached to idols. When we give ourselves to an idol, whether an Omega watch or images of naked women, we make ourselves vulnerable to the Enemy. Obviously, an Omega watch and a beautiful woman aren't inherently evil, but what we do with them determines whether or not they constitute an idol.

Idolatry, however, operates like a two-for-one deal. When you pick up an idol, Satan throws in a demon for good measure. It's like propositioning a prostitute only to find out she's an undercover cop. Similarly, our sexual addictions give the powers of darkness the right to act as squatters in our hearts. We didn't give them permission to occupy that space, but our illicit sexual behaviors act as a vacancy sign that says, "Free room and board!" And once we grant the powers of darkness permission to influence us, the Enemy uses two important strategies to further deepen our bondage: footholds and strongholds.

## FOOTHOLDS ARE DOORWAYS TO DARKNESS

In Ephesians 4:26–27 Paul wrote, "In your anger do not sin: Do not let the sun go down while you are still angry, and do not give the devil a foothold." Was Paul suggesting that anger is the only sin that gives the devil a foothold? Was he saying that anger is something so pernicious that the devil uses it like nothing else? I doubt it.

In fact, considering his context—he was writing about transformation from the old self to the new self—he seemed to use anger as an illustration of how Satan uses sin in general as an entry point into our lives. Paul very well could have said, "In your anxiety, in your lust, in your passivity, do not sin . . . and do not give the devil a foothold."

This tells us that small and seemingly unrelated issues like anger can open the door to sin, which in turn can open the door to the Enemy's influence. Here's what it has looked like for me. One moment I'm slightly irritated with my wife for leaving the cupboard doors open. When I indulge that irritation, her habit of leaving cupboard doors open becomes a personal attack against me, and suddenly, I am a helpless victim in my marriage. Now I am angry and want to make her pay!

In his book *Disarming the Darkness*, Calvin Miller gave a spot-on description of the Enemy's tactics with footholds: "He rarely comes to us asking us to sign a contract for our souls. He is rather the god of the side deals, who never buys souls all at once. He purchases us on the installment plan."[3]

## STRONGHOLDS ARE DWELLING PLACES FOR DARKNESS

If a foothold opens the door to darkness, then what is a stronghold? The word itself means a fortress, a place that is heavily defended against the enemy. During World War II, when the Allied forces landed on Omaha Beach, they battled reinforced strongholds defended by the enemy army that had already conquered Europe.

Spiritually speaking, certain circumstances allow the Enemy to not only get in the door but also set up camp and stay for a while, all with the goal of conquering the individual. Paul described the nature of our war against the Enemy's strongholds this way: "For though we live in the world, we do not wage war as the world does. The weapons we fight with are not the weapons of the world. On the contrary, they have divine power to demolish strongholds. We demolish arguments and every pretension that sets itself up against the knowledge of God, and we take captive every thought to make it obedient to Christ" (2 Cor. 10:3–5).

Notice that Paul began with the assumption that believers are actively engaged in a war. He also reminded us that our weapons in this battle are distinctly different from the world's weapons. Also, notice that Paul defined *strongholds* as "arguments" and "pretension"—*beliefs and lies*—that take root in us, and that stand in the way of knowing God. These falsehoods concern our perceptions about God, ourselves, or others.

Lastly, notice the order of the warfare. Strongholds are demolished before every thought is taken captive. Countless men have told me that they cannot control, or take captive, their thoughts. But we cannot take our thoughts captive, or overcome any other sexual sin, until the stronghold has been demolished.

When the U.S. Navy Seals captured and killed Osama bin Laden, they didn't walk up to his compound, ring the doorbell, and quietly request that Mr. Bin Laden come with them. Instead, they commandeered the heavily defended compound in which he had been living before taking his life. It works the same way in the spiritual sense.

## DEMOLISHING FOOTHOLDS AND STRONGHOLDS IN YOUR LIFE

The good news is, the footholds and strongholds in your life can be removed. James 4:7 tells us, "Submit yourselves, then, to God. Resist the devil, and he will flee." Submitting to God and resisting the devil are not one action. We cannot submit to God and resist the devil at the same time. But something as simple as submitting to God places us in the position to begin destroying lifelong footholds and strongholds.

At the risk of sounding formulaic, three necessary steps are required to demolish footholds and strongholds in your life. First, you must *announce* the lie you have befriended. Below are some of the most common ones.

- *I will never be sexually satisfied in my marriage.*
- *Sexual gratification is necessary for my well-being.*
- *I will always be ruled by lust and cannot change.*
- *Real intimacy is not worth the risk.*
- *I don't really love God or I wouldn't be struggling this way.*
- *My heart must be desperately wicked.*
- *I can never let anyone know my deepest struggles.*
- *I am not a strong and powerful man.*

Ask God to reveal to you the lies that you believe. You may want to echo the psalmist's prayer in Psalm 43:3: "Send me your light and your truth, let them guide me."

Once you've identified the lie, then you must announce it. Nowhere does the Bible say that you must say it out loud, but Scripture seems to indicate that we exercise our God-given authority when we speak the lie out loud. When Jesus sent out seventy-two of His followers in Luke 10 to minister on His behalf, they were astonished that the demons submitted to them. "Lord," they exclaimed, "even the demons submit to us in your name" (v. 17). In order for the demons to submit *in the name of Jesus*, the name of Jesus needed to be invoked. Something powerful takes place when we speak out truth in Jesus' name.

Next, you must *renounce* the lie. In 2 Corinthians 4:2 Paul declared that he had "renounced . . . shameful ways." He didn't say that he'd stopped them, or even repented of them. He said "renounced." Renouncing means to formally withdraw from participating in the lie, like a gang member who renounces his affiliation in a gang. You may have believed the lie in your past, but you are deciding—by an act of your will—that you will no longer buy into it.

False beliefs, lies, and accusations from the Enemy can be difficult to renounce because at some level they helped protect our hearts. For example, when I believed the lie that nobody would love me for who I actually was, I couldn't risk being vulnerable enough to receive my wife's love for me. I pushed her away or sabotaged our relationship whenever she got too close. That lie dies hard. Consistent persistence is the key.

Finally, we must *pronounce* the truth. As you intend to pronounce the truth, a Scripture may come to mind or you may hear God speak the truth about you. At this point in the prayer, I encourage men to ask, "Jesus, what do You want to say to me?" or,

"Jesus, what truth do You have to speak to me?" or, "Jesus, what is true about me?" You can run the lie by Him by asking God, "Am I a loser?"

## A PRAYER FOR BREAKING SEXUAL STRONGHOLDS[4]

The following prayer is similar to ones I began praying shortly after I experienced the violent sexual images that I mentioned at the beginning of the chapter. I know many people who have prayed this prayer on a regular basis during certain seasons of their lives. It's not a onetime shot, where you pray it, and—POOF!—no more struggle. But it best represents a way of surrendering your sexual brokenness, your good heart, and your life to the lordship of Christ. And it helps familiarize you with the language and principles of spiritual warfare.

> Lord Jesus Christ, I confess here and now that You are my Creator [John 1:3] and therefore the Creator of my sexuality. I confess that You are also my Savior, that You have ransomed me with Your blood [Matt. 20:28; 1 Cor. 15:3]. I have been bought with the blood of Jesus Christ; my life and my body belong to God [1 Cor. 6:19–20]. Jesus, I present myself to You now to be made whole and holy in every way, including in my sexuality. You ask us to present our bodies to You as living sacrifices [Rom. 12:1] and the parts of our bodies as instruments of righteousness [Rom. 6:13]. I do this now. I present my body, my sexuality, and my sexual nature to You.
>
> Jesus, I ask Your Holy Spirit to help me now remember, confess, and renounce my sexual sins. [Pause. Listen. Remember. Confess and renounce.] Lord Jesus, I ask Your forgiveness for every act of sexual sin. You promised that if we confess our sins, You are faithful and just to forgive us our sins and cleanse us from all unrighteousness

[1 John 1:9]. *I ask You to cleanse me of my sexual sins now; cleanse my body, soul, and spirit; cleanse my heart and mind and will; cleanse my sexuality. Thank You for forgiving me and cleansing me. I receive Your forgiveness and cleansing. I renounce every claim I have given Satan to my life or sexuality through my sexual sins. Those claims are now broken by the cross and blood of Jesus Christ* [Col. 2:13–15].

*Lord Jesus, I thank You for offering me total and complete forgiveness. I receive that forgiveness now. I choose to forgive myself for all of my sexual wrongdoing. I also choose to forgive those who have harmed me sexually.* [Be specific here; name those people, and forgive them.] *I release them to You. I release all my anger and judgment toward them. Come, Lord Jesus, into the pain they caused me, and heal me with Your love.*

*I now bring the cross of my Lord Jesus Christ between me and every person with whom I have been sexually intimate.* [Name them specifically whenever possible. Also, name those who have abused you sexually.] *I break all sexual, emotional, and spiritual bonds with* [name, if possible]. *I keep the cross of Christ between us.*

*I renounce* [name the struggle—"the inability to have an orgasm" or "this lingering shame" or "the hatred of my body" or "this lack of desire"]. *I bring the cross and blood of Jesus Christ against this* [guilt or shame, every negative consequence]. *Lord Jesus, I also ask You to reveal to me any agreements I have made about my sexuality or this specific struggle.* [An example would be "I will always struggle with this" or "I don't deserve to enjoy sex now" or "My sexuality is dirty." Pause and let Jesus reveal those agreements to you. Then break them.] *I break this agreement* [name it] *in the name of my Lord Jesus Christ, and I renounce every claim I have given it in my life.*

*Lord Jesus, I now consecrate my sexuality to You in every way. I consecrate my sexual intimacy with my spouse to You. I ask You to cleanse and heal my sexuality and our sexual intimacy in every way.*

*I ask Your healing grace to come and free me from all consequences of sexual sin. I ask You to fill my sexuality with Your healing love and goodness. Restore my sexuality in wholeness. Let my spouse and me both experience all of the intimacy and pleasure You intended a man and woman to enjoy in marriage. I pray all of this in the name of Jesus Christ my Lord. Amen.*

Pray this alone, pray it with your spouse, pastor, counselor . . . but just pray it! Be strong; take courage. The Enemy may be lying to you right now and saying that this is hokey or kooky, but don't listen to him. The more you "hear" you shouldn't pray this, the more you need to get on your knees and pray right now. And keep praying every day until you are totally and completely free.

# Your Brain on Porn

Like sand on a beach, the brain bears the footprints of
the decisions we have made, the skills we have learned
**—SHARON BEGLEY, *NEWSWEEK* SCIENCE EDITOR**[1]

Restart and reboot yourself. You're free to go.
**—U2, "UNKNOWN CALLER"**[2]

"I know it's not really true," said Manny, "but it seems as if my brain has been conditioned by porn. I've tried everything and nothing helps."

"Why do you say it's not really true?" I asked.

"It's like saying, 'It's not really my fault,'" he answered. "I can't blame anyone or anything else for my problem. I'm supposed to trust God, right?"

"What if your brain *really is* conditioned to need porn?" I asked. "And what if acknowledging that meant that you were actually exercising faith?"

"Well, that would be pretty cool," he said, chuckling. "I wouldn't feel like such an absolute loser."

My conversation with Manny is not unlike talks I've had with many men who have sincerely pursued recovering from porn addiction but who have not yet realized that porn physically changes the brain. Without understanding porn's impact on the brain, too many men either quit trying to change or carry unnecessary guilt and shame when their spiritual zeal and willpower aren't enough.

Any discussion about compulsive use of pornography is incomplete without understanding these physical changes. God created human beings in physical bodies, and David wrote of his own creation in the womb that he was "fearfully and wonderfully made" (Ps. 139:14). So are we. Defining ourselves and our problems in only spiritual terms not only is unbiblical but also hinders our recovery.

In the last decade, the field of neuroscience has exploded our understanding of the human brain. Recent discoveries have profound implications on treating various addictions and psychological disorders, and pursuing physical and emotional well-being. The consistent theme is that contrary to conventional wisdom, our brains are highly changeable.

When you fly on a major airline, your journey begins with a preflight announcement, which includes a review of the emergency procedure card in the back pocket in the seat in front of you. That card gives you important instructions about how to escape to safety in the event of emergency. You aren't asked to master the finer details of airplane safety; you're given basic instructions that could save your life if something goes wrong. My goal in this chapter is to give you the back-pocket version of how porn affects your brain, and how you can use this information to break free from porn's grip on your brain.

Back in the day, a popular public service announcement on television touted the dangers of drug use. "This is drugs," a man began, as the screen showed a sizzling skillet. "This is your brain on drugs," the voice-over continued, as an egg is cracked into the hot skillet and is instantly fried. "Any questions?" the PSA concludes.[3] Its meaning is clear. Behavioral addictions, like porn, affect the brain just like drugs—in all major respects.[4]

## YOUR MOST IMPORTANT SEX ORGAN

If you were to ask a random man on the street to name his most important sex organ, the answer would be predictable. But sexual desire and arousal do not begin in the genitals. As you will see, a man's most important sex organ is his brain. Therefore, when changes occur in parts of the brain related to sex, it also changes his sexual desire and his ability to choose how to act upon it.

Okay, here comes the technical stuff. "The human brain is a wet, coconut-sized, walnut-shaped organ, the color of raw liver and the consistency of an overripe peach."[5] Lovely description, isn't it? Which makes it hard to imagine that within this mysterious structure are ten to twenty billion cells called *neurons*, each interconnected in a complex set of neuropathways. Between each neuron is a space—just one-millionth of an inch—called a *synapse*—where electrochemicals known as *neurotransmitters* serve as information couriers. Think of the chemicals as the "message" or "words" and the receptors on the receiving nerve cells as the "ears."

The brain is composed of numerous regions and substructures, each assigned a specific function. The two largest regions in the brain are the *limbic system* and the *cerebral cortex*. Want a simple visual? Hold your hand out, palm down. Now fold your thumb in toward your palm, and make a fist. The cerebral cortex is represented by the outer part of your fist, while the enfolded thumb in the middle of your fist represents the limbic system. For the rest of the chapter, when I refer to these structures, think fist and thumb.

The limbic system, sometimes referred to as the *inner brain*, or the *primitive brain*, governs emotions like fear, joy, and sadness. It also controls our hunger and thirst, sexual drives and urges, motivation, and basic survival instincts. When a child touches a hot stove, the limbic system reacts and the child learns, *Not good to touch hot stove!* When that frightened child runs into the arms of a loving parent, the limbic system reacts and the child learns, *This is good!* The limbic system is largely instinctual, with little rational or logical ability, and no understanding of consequences or actions.

The cerebral cortex, sometimes called the *outer brain*, is the seat of awareness, perception, and thought. It governs the logical part of the brain that allows for planning, executing, reflecting, and decision making. The cerebral cortex (along with the limbic system) is involved in morality, understanding the consequences of certain actions, and impulse control.[6] This part of the brain in nonaddicted people prevents actions they might later regret.

If you remember nothing else about the brain as it relates to porn, remember the chemical neurotransmitter dopamine. Known as the "gotta have it" molecule and the "I want it" molecule, it has been described by one brain expert as the gas that fuels our desire engine.[7] This neurotransmitter involves anticipation and expectation. When we imagine eating at a favorite restaurant, shopping for a new gadget, or having sex, the brain releases dopamine, and our senses call out, *Gimme, gimme, gimme.* The more intense the experience, the more dopamine is released in the brain.

When a man looks at porn, dopamine levels rise, causing a heightened sense of excitement. Conversely, when dopamine levels drop, the excitement level drops. Without this neurotransmitter, we would stay in bed all day with no motivation to eat or pursue meaningful goals, relationships, or sexual pleasure. Dopamine is *the* neurotransmitter behind all motivation.

## PORN CAN OVERSTIMULATE YOUR BRAIN

If some malevolent being held a competition to create the perfect delivery mechanism to enslave our human desire, Internet pornography would win the grand prize. You must understand that online pornography is fundamentally different from the *Playboy*s or

*Penthouses* of past generations. If the magazines, videos, and DVDs of the past were like the Wright brothers' plane at Kitty Hawk, then Internet porn would be a supersonic jet. Although supersonic jets are impressive for military use or high-speed travel, you wouldn't want one landing in your backyard. But this is the impact Internet porn makes on the brain. Its sheer power and intensity create a heightened level of stimulation that your brain was never intended to experience. Because of this, the brain of a man regularly using porn can change and shape itself to resemble neuropathways similar to those of an alcoholic or drug addict.[8]

Much of what is written on the relationship between compulsive porn use and the brain emphasizes the addictive power of orgasm. No one would argue that the orgasm is one of the most powerful physical, emotional—and some would say spiritual—experiences of being alive. Scientists have shown that in those moments of ecstasy and surrender, the release of serotonin, dopamine, oxytocin, and norepinephrine is as powerful in the brain as heroin.[9] But what, then, makes porn so different from having sex or masturbating? The answer will surprise you.

Internet porn overstimulates the brain. This occurs in four unique ways. First, our brains crave novelty, and the Internet provides an endless variety of novel sexual images. When I was a young man looking at magazine centerfolds, images lost their appeal within a short amount of time. But with online porn, new images are instantly available with the click of a mouse. With each new image, our limbic system releases a burst of dopamine, which tells us we *gotta have it.*

The connection between novelty and sexual arousal is well established by what scientists call the *Coolidge effect.*[10] After dropping a male rat into a cage with a receptive female, researchers initially observed intense copulation between the rats. Eventually, the male rat exhausted himself; even when the willing female rat wanted more, he was spent. However, when the original female was replaced with a *new receptive female*, the male rat immediately revived and began to copulate again. This pattern was repeated over and over until the male rat was literally exhausted. With the introduction of a novel sexual mate, this process will be repeated again and again until the male succumbs to exhaustion or death.

In the real world, even Hugh Hefner doesn't enjoy an endless supply of women to revive his sexual capacities at any given time. But in the unreal world of online porn, new and ever more stimulating "mates" provide complete novelty without ever needing to step away from the computer. As long as the novelty continues, the arousal continues—while dopamine fuels the desire engine. One man I recently spoke with averaged six hours a day viewing porn. In his case, every click on a new image released more dopamine, which inflamed his desire. You can see already that a vicious cycle is set in place.

A second reason why Internet porn overstimulates the brain is that it provides no limits on the amount we can consume. In food and substance addictions, a person either runs out of the drug or food, or is physically unable to tolerate more. A man can eat only so many pizzas or smoke only so much crack before reaching the obvious limits. With Internet porn, an infinite supply is available. And as long as a man has an Internet connection, he can continue to binge. This is why it's not uncommon for addicted men to stay up all night viewing porn, and even lose track of time.

The third reason Internet porn overstimulates the brain deals with tolerance. Tolerance occurs when a person needs more of the substance or activity to get the same effect. Over time, we grow increasingly tolerant to certain stimulants. With drugs and food, tolerance typically means eating more frequently or consuming larger amounts. With Internet porn, a man can overcome the tolerance effect two ways. He can increase the amount by spending more time viewing porn. Or he can overcome his tolerance by escalating the intensity of the images he sees. That's why men often move from the *Sports Illustrated* swimsuit issue to soft porn to hardcore porn to degradation, bestiality, rape, or other scenes typically deemed repulsive and shocking. They do this not because they are predisposed to it, but because the strong emotions of shock, disgust, or shame provide the sought-after dopamine burst. Gravitating toward aberrant sexual behavior becomes the only way to get a fix.

Finally, Internet porn overstimulates the brain because it's available on demand. Again, unlike substances that require the user to arrange for a fix, a man carries a forever stash of porn in his mind without even turning on the computer. Every time the images come to mind, he experiences a burst of dopamine in his neuropathways. Combine these four factors and you have a perfect storm brewing in the neurochemical sea of the brain. Over time, the brain is physically changed, and the man becomes addicted to his own brain chemistry.

## OVERSTIMULATING YOUR BRAIN CAUSES YOUR BRAIN TO CHANGE

Many men relate that after ongoing porn use they become increasingly frustrated. Apart from conscience or conviction, why is this the case? Every addiction occurs because the brain has adapted to being overstimulated—too much dopamine. As a result, three troublesome changes occur in the brain. The first of these involves our cravings. Cravings occur when dopamine (the "I want it" neurotransmitter) is released. When more dopamine is released, a man experiences cravings. Cravings usually lead to viewing more porn. Viewing more porn leads to more dopamine being released. More dopamine leads to viewing more porn. You get the picture. It's a potentially never-ending cycle. But cravings are only one-third of the problem.

In the center of the limbic system (the center of our urges and desires) there is a reward circuit flowing to the cerebral cortex—the rational part of the brain. Ideally, this circuit works in harmony. When the limbic system urges you to have another piece of chocolate cake, the cerebral cortex reminds you that you can't fit into your jeans, so you say, "No, thanks." In the case of a man whose brain is not yet addicted to porn, his limbic system may urge him to Google the words "naked women," but his cerebral cortex reminds him that his wife or girlfriend may not think highly of such an act. Porn, however, throws the reward circuit off balance. Rather than complete the circuit in harmony, porn trips the circuit breaker, and disharmony occurs between the two systems.

What does this look like? When the "go for it" system is overloaded with excess dopamine, the "think about it" system responds by saying, *System overload!* and shuts down. Think about it this way. Across the synapse—the microspace between neurons—reward cells talk to one another through dopamine signaling. Dopamine, remember, is the message, and the receptors on the receiving nerve cells are the ears.

When dopamine is released in large amounts or for long periods, two things happen simultaneously. First, the receiving nerve cells get overstimulated and start removing receptors. It's like when someone keeps shouting at you; you cover your ears. But the sending cells scream even louder (more dopamine) until they are hoarse, and can now only whisper (the amount of dopamine sent is below normal). With the receiving cells half deaf (fewer receptors) and the sending cells whispering (less dopamine released), you are left with two options—feeling awful, or finding porn, the one thing that now releases dopamine more than anything else. With porn this is a gradual process, yet it lies at the heart of addiction. Low dopamine signaling that leads to a numbed pleasure response is known as *desensitization*. It is precisely why men feel so helpless, so powerless, when they try to overcome their sexual addictions.

In 1942 C. S. Lewis wrote *The Screwtape Letters*, a story about a senior demon named Screwtape who instructs a junior demon named Wormwood in the wiles of evil. "An ever-increasing craving for an ever-diminishing pleasure is the formula," Screwtape advises. "It is more certain; and it's better style. To get the man's soul and give him nothing in return—that is what really gladdens our Father's [Satan's] heart."[11]

Even in Lewis's vivid imagination, I'm almost certain he never envisioned MRI machines and PET scanners, which today support his theological idea.

## PORN REWIRES YOUR BRAIN . . .

Every thought, feeling, habit, skill, or behavior in your life has a corresponding neuropathway that fires in your brain. These pathways are designed to function optimally. However, as the brain's reward circuitry gets entangled in a tug-of-war, the brain rewires itself for addiction and new neuropathways are created. Every time a man views porn, or eventually even thinks about porn, the burst of dopamine strengthens the connections between cells. The stronger the connection, the easier it becomes for cells to communicate on that path. This idea of the brain changing itself is called *neuroplasticity*. Whether learning to ski, learning to speak a foreign language, or looking at porn, the more we use a neuropathway, the more our brain changes, making the pathway stronger.

These neuropathways are like footpaths across a field of waist-high grass. Walking across the field when the grass is so high requires significant effort. But each time you walk along the path, it gets easier. The grass is trampled and worn down, and it eventually becomes a dirt path.

As our brains are rewired, porn works like a Weed eater cutting through the tall grass. Porn becomes the path of least resistance in the brain. And the easier the path, the more likely we are to take it, even when we don't want to. The creation of this path of least resistance is called *sensitization*.

## . . . BUT YOU CAN REBOOT IT!

But we have good news. Our brains can be rewired from their addictive patterns. Just as you can reboot your computer and reset the hard drive, you can reboot your brain and restore the sensitivity of your brain circuits. On a computer it's as simple as pressing the power button or clicking a pull-down menu to restart. But rebooting your brain may be the most difficult thing you've ever done.

Jessie didn't think he could exist without porn. When I met him, he had been viewing porn daily for many years. Most days he watched porn and then masturbated in bed. He couldn't fall asleep without it. Today Jessie lives porn-free and enjoys a life he never thought possible. To be able to reboot like he did, you will need a map to help you reach your destination. Here are some practical instructions as you begin the journey.

### Define Your Objective and Prepare

I know countless men who listen to a talk about sexual integrity or attend a men's retreat and then make a sincere, though emotional, attempt to break the "lather, rinse, repeat" cycle. This is commendable. However, recent behavioral research supports the Boy Scout motto—"Be prepared." You're more likely to succeed in changing your addictive or compulsive behaviors when you take time to define a clear objective and prepare yourself for the changes you will be making. People who identify the problem and impulsively take action, without planning ahead, are far more likely to experience relapse.

How do you prepare? First, *define your objective*. Rebooting your brain does not make a worthy end goal and will not give you lasting freedom or long-term transformation. The purpose of rebooting is to create a "time-out" so your brain can begin to regain balance. Only when this happens can any longer-term changes take place. You can't overhaul a car engine unless the motor is turned off. Rebooting is like turning off the engine so the real work can begin. A man I recently spoke with who was in the middle of the rebooting process defined his objective as "becoming a strong, transparent, involved husband and father, while pursuing a life of integrity." His objective went beyond rebooting to the kind of person he wanted to become.

Second, prepare yourself, and then begin your first *ninety days of abstinence*. Porn has insulated you from your life. As you reboot, many of the feelings you've avoided through porn may rise to the surface. An old bumper sticker from the '70s reads, "Reality is for those who can't handle drugs." As you begin to live in a reality without porn, you may experience a wide variety of feelings, thoughts, and regrets.

During the first two weeks of abstinence, you may suffer intense withdrawal symptoms that may come and go. These can include fatigue, depression, difficulty concentrating, tension, nervousness, sleeplessness, headaches, increase (or decrease) in sexual arousal, increased appetite for food, rapid heartbeat, shortness of breath, and itchy skin. In more extreme cases withdrawal symptoms may include shakes, nausea, and panic or anxiety. Preparing for this empowers you, reminding you that this stage won't last. In most situations symptoms last roughly two weeks. Of course, consult a physician with any troubling concerns.

Third, prepare yourself for *cravings*. The presence of cravings does not mean you are, as Manny said, "an absolute loser." Remember, cravings result from overstimulation of your brain. You can resist cravings in a number of ways that I will describe in chapter 12.

Fourth, be prepared for *relapse*—a return to porn and masturbation. Relapse does not have to be seen as failure; it can be an important opportunity for learning. Holding on to the idea that you won't, or can't, relapse is not only unrealistic; it's counterproductive. If you fall, get back up. Some people hear the drama of my story and assume that I experienced an immediate breakthrough. But my journey from identifying my addiction to freedom took four years.

### Don't Walk Alone

You can't do this by yourself. Ask a friend to meet with you on a regular basis for prayer and encouragement. Ideally, you will benefit from participating in a group or workshop designed to help people with addictive and compulsive behavior. This person, group, or program ought to be a source of accountability, which I discuss in chapter 14.

### Set a Start Date

Determine the day you will commit yourself to sexual sobriety. Once you begin, keep a calendar to track the days, weeks, and months. Initially, this can serve as a big motivator to monitor and celebrate your progress. If you fall, it's not the end. You are continuously and simultaneously rewiring the porn pathways and willpower pathways in your brain. It's like two pathways of grass. Every time you refuse to yield to your cravings, grass grows a little bit on the porn pathways, and you trample the grass on the willpower pathways in your frontal cortex. One weakens as the other strengthens.

The amount of time it takes to rewire the brain varies from

person to person, but you may begin to experience changes in as early as ninety days or during the rebooting process. Ultimately, rewiring is a long-term process determined by many factors, including abstinence, core beliefs, self-care, and level of addiction.

### Pull the Trigger

Learn to live without porn by abstaining from pornography and masturbation. I know: you've tried this before, and it hasn't worked. That's okay. This time you will be armed with the knowledge that in the short term you are seeking to change your brain, not just flex your volitional muscles.

### Work to Maintain Your Abstinence

Addicts and alcoholics have a saying: "My trouble isn't stopping; my problem is staying stopped." Rebooting your brain is not the end point; it's the launching point. Once you no longer feel compelled to view porn, you can follow God's path for your life. This is addressed in chapter 12 as I discuss the soul care cycle.

## HOW TO REWIRE YOUR BRAIN

One of the most profound discoveries in understanding the brain involves the concept of *neuroplasticity*. This is the idea that our brain changes as the result of experience. Porn changes the brain in an undesirable way. The man who doesn't watch porn, or is not yet addicted, has yet to develop sensitized "weed-whacked" pathways. But the porn neuropathways of a man whose brain is addicted are weed-whacked and trampled down so that they have become the path of least resistance. But your brain can be changed in a positive and healthy direction. Rewiring your brain allows it to unlearn the addictive patterns and relearn impulse control. This occurs as the addictive "gotta have it" pathways are weakened and the "think about it" pathways are strengthened. Here's how you can begin rewiring your brain.

### Practice Intentional Thinking

What you think about is ultimately what you become. What we once called "the power of positive thinking" is increasingly backed by scientific evidence. The more attention your brain pays to a given input, the stronger and more elaborately it will be wired and retained in the brain.[12] When we give our attention and focus to good things, like peace, joy, and self-control, our brains rewire themselves in a way that allows us to experience those good things. Wouldn't it make sense, then, to be intentional about what we give ourselves to?

With this in mind, consider the words of the apostle Paul: "Finally, brothers and sisters, whatever is true, whatever is noble, whatever is right, whatever is pure, whatever is lovely, whatever is admirable—if anything is excellent or praiseworthy—think about such things" (Phil. 4:8 UPDATED NIV).

When Scripture exhorts us to set our minds on good things, it concerns more than just the well-being of our souls. It also affects the well-being of our brains. Our neural circuitry forms itself around whatever we give our attention and focus to. That's why Paul connected our transformation with the renewing of our minds: "Do not conform to the pattern of this world, but be transformed by the renewing of your mind" (Rom. 12:2).

In the next chapter I discuss how you can practice focusing on what is pure, lovely, and admirable, in a way that rewires your brain to its original setting before porn—but better.

### Pursue Alternate Passions

The famous philosopher, novelist, and poet Johann Wolfgang von Goethe was right. We are shaped and fashioned by what we love. Certainly this applies to our brains. The life focus of a man struggling with porn leads to tunnel vision. When a man views porn on a regular basis, his passions are held captive, and he forfeits the ability to direct his life in the way he would otherwise choose.

Many men realize the importance of pursuing their passions. What is life-giving to your soul? What relationships have been affected by your use of porn? What enjoyable activities have stopped? Of all possible alternative passions, exercise is the most crucial. Studies show that exercise increases dopamine receptors, therefore helping to rewire the brain.[13] Another study showed that the number one behavior associated with successful substance abuse recovery was exercise.[14] If you have not been physically active in the past with some form of exercise, it's important that you begin. Don't assume you have to join a health club or sign up for the Ironman Triathlon. You can walk, hike, or ride a bike. Take the stairs instead of the elevator.

Recent attention has been given to children and adults who suffer from NDD, or *nature deficit disorder*, as a result of spending too much time online or engaged in electronic media. Avoid this disorder by interacting with the outdoors in the sunshine, fresh air, and natural beauty of God's creation. Get out and move! Pursuing alternative passions expands your horizons and rewires your brain at the same time.

### Employ the Power of Repetition

Studies show that repeated behaviors, over time, cause structural changes in the brain. These changes can be negative—causing compulsion and addiction. Or they can be positive—rewiring the brain so the stimuli of porn and lust are no longer a reflexive reaction. Repetition helps lock behaviors in the brain in the same way an athlete develops muscle memory. Or consider a concert pianist. When performing, he never thinks, *Now I will reach my left hand exactly seven inches to the right while simultaneously moving my right hand two inches to the left.* Instead, the pianist's brain has learned to bypass the conscious cognitive step and follow a learned response.

So be encouraged. Your struggle with porn is a learned response, in many ways, just like the skills of a pianist or athlete. Your brain can unlearn, and it *can* change.[15]

11

# Less Is More

In repentance and rest is your salvation, in quietness and
trust is your strength, but you would have none of it.

—THE SOVEREIGN LORD[1]

It was the kind of morning that was sure to light the fuse of my lust
and preoccupation. I overslept and ran late for a breakfast meeting.
My good intentions were to wake up early to an unhurried morning, enjoy a cup of coffee, and begin my day with a full tank. But
running late, I raced through the shower, dressed, and headed out
the door. I was oblivious to the eight inches of snow that had fallen
during the night. Because I hadn't gotten around to cleaning the
garage, my car sat in the driveway all night, with the windshield
covered in a sheet of ice. Stressed-out, I started to beat myself up for
not cleaning the garage. So I reached for the ice scraper in the back
of my car. It wasn't there.

Because I was running late, I opened my wallet and pulled out
my driver's license. It is a little-known fact that this handy piece
of government-issued plastic—only two and a half by three and a
half inches—doubles as an ice scraper. After ten minutes my hands
were nearly frostbitten, but the windshield was spotless. My window
now clean, I jumped into my car and unconsciously turned on the
radio. I wanted something that would cut through the deafening

silence. Back and forth I pushed the preprogrammed buttons, hoping to hear something that would breathe life into my impoverished soul. *World-class rock—no, that's not it. Classic rock—not quite. Oldies station—nope. How about something positive and encouraging? Not feeling very positive or encouraged. News or talk radio?* Nothing seemed to hit the spot in my frantic search to calm the stress and fill the void. When I arrived at my meeting twenty minutes late, I had already become preoccupied with when and how I could act out again sexually.

## WE ARE TERRIFIED OF BEING WITH OURSELVES

Blaise Pascal once wrote that all human troubles can be distilled down to the single idea that we can't spend an hour alone with ourselves in a room. This explains why the first thing I do after turning the key to start my car is reach for my iPhone or turn on the radio. Other men I know repeat the same story.

Being alone with ourselves can generate reactions ranging from mild distractedness to outright panic. A line from the Counting Crows song "Perfect Blue Buildings" reflects our aversion to being alone: "Gotta get me a little oblivion, baby. How am I gonna keep myself away from me?"[2] When we are alone, we encounter everything we have tried so hard to avoid. We face the emotional, relational, and spiritual noise that has been kept at bay by counterfeit good and counterfeit truth.

It seems odd to say that we are averse to being with ourselves, much less with God. But we have become, as Kierkegaard said, tranquilized by the trivial. When the tranquilizer wears off and the analgesics of busyness and distraction lie beyond our reach, we have no other option but to face our inner worlds. In the twenty-first century there is no task more difficult, no spiritual discipline more painful, than learning to be still. But there is none more rewarding.

Let's be blunt. If you are going to seriously address your issue with porn and lust, you must come to terms with the restlessness and turmoil in your soul. The feelings and experiences within you are manifestations of your brokenness. Where there is chaos, anxiety, tension, loneliness, disappointment, sadness, shame, drivenness, dividedness—whatever it may be—brokenness is calling you. Calling you to pay attention to it. And only after you have paid attention to it, to yield it to God.

## FACE THE EMPTINESS IN YOUR SOUL

When I was single and my addiction was most out of control, I worked the 3:00–11:00 p.m. shift at a hospital. Most of the time I wouldn't get to bed before 2:00 a.m. When I woke up the next day, between 9:00 and 10:00 a.m., my roommate and other friends were already working their day jobs. The loneliness and emptiness I felt during that season felt like a gaping hole in the center of my being.

But always the schemer, I had a solution to deal with it. Every morning, though I couldn't afford it, I went out to breakfast at a local diner. The diner was a place where I was known. Every morning, the owner and his ever-maternal waitress, Stella, greeted me. Stella always welcomed me with a smile and placed her hand on my shoulder while she poured my coffee. I still remember the warmth of her touch. For just a moment each morning, it soothed the emptiness in my soul.

In a recent conversation with my spiritual director, I asked why, even now, solitude can be so difficult for me. "When you are empty, being alone with yourself is almost always a scary thing," he said. "But when you are full, it is almost always a joy—like being with a good friend." I never thought of it that way. It wasn't being alone I was afraid of; it was emptiness. And the many cracks in the cup of my soul explained the reason my cup didn't remain full. The emptiness that led me to meals I couldn't afford at the diner was the very same emptiness that led me to porn and prostitutes.

Dealing with our emptiness is one of the most difficult legs on our journey from addiction to freedom. As Henri Nouwen explained, our only choice is to face it head-on: "To live a spiritual life we must first find the courage to enter into the desert of our loneliness and to change it by gentle and persistent efforts into a garden of solitude. The movement from loneliness to solitude, however, is the beginning of any spiritual life because it is the movement from the restless senses to the restful spirit, from the outward-reaching cravings to the inward-reaching search, from the fearful clinging to the fearless play."[3]

Any man who has struggled with lust and porn can relate to Nouwen's "restless senses," "outward-reaching cravings," and "fearful clinging." However, the restful spirit of which he wrote is no "pie in the sky" spiritual ideal reserved for monks and a select few with too much time on their hands. Not only is a restful soul within reach; it is a crucial component of the "living encounter with God" described by Tim Keller.[4] But how do we begin to cross from the emptiness of loneliness to the fulfillment of solitude?

## TRANSFORM THE EMPTINESS IN YOUR SOUL

For many years after breaking free from my addiction, I cringed at the words "spiritual disciplines." For me, the very idea of spiritual disciplines evoked images of sin management and rolling up my sleeves to repair my moral depravity. For too long I believed that if I could simply be disciplined enough spiritually, then I could grasp God in such a way that together we would turn off the faucet of sin.

Today when I hear the words "spiritual disciplines," I feel joy. I've discovered that spiritual disciplines are not about trying to be more spiritual, or grasping for God to get something from Him. Instead, I like to think of spiritual disciplines as a way of allowing God to grasp me. They help me create space in my life to be attentive to the life within, so I can hear His voice.

For men struggling with porn, the most important spiritual practices are the disciplines of solitude and silence. Through solitude we learn the practice of intentionally being alone. Through silence we learn the practice of being quiet. Together, solitude and silence build a foundation that allows us to listen to our own lives and to listen to the voice of God.

Solitude and silence are critical in our hyper-connected world. With the constant barrage of information and communication, it's virtually impossible to turn off the noise and busyness without being intentional. Not long ago I realized that by keeping my iPhone on my nightstand, I was checking my e-mail before I even got out of bed. Discovering that something so insignificant had ensnared my soul truly humbled me.

Don't be misled. When we shut off our electronic gadgets and turn away from the distractions, we don't automatically step into some spiritually idyllic world of peace, joy, and contentment. I wish it were that easy. More often, when we unplug, our internal distractedness confronts us, making us wonder if we suffer from spiritual attention deficit disorder. Nouwen got it when he wrote:

> Entering a private room and shutting the door, therefore, does not mean that we immediately shut out all our inner doubts, anxieties, fears, bad memories, unresolved conflicts, angry feelings and impulsive desires. On the contrary, when we have removed our outer distraction, we often find that our inner distractions manifest themselves to us in full force. We often use

the outer distractions to shield ourselves from the interior noises. This makes the discipline of solitude all the more important.[5]

Solitude and silence are not just practices to optimize our lives in a fast-paced world. And though these practices may bring us healing, they are far more than a trendy therapeutic technique. Our souls require solitude and silence in order to thrive. Jesus, who lived in a low-tech culture, regularly practiced solitude and silence. Who better to learn from than the Master?

Before Jesus kicked off His ministry, He spent forty days in the solitude of the desert (Matt. 4:1–2). Often, before ministering or preaching, He woke up early in the morning and retreated to a solitary place to pray (Mark 1:35–39). When Jesus heard that John the Baptist was beheaded, He withdrew by a boat to a solitary place (Matt. 14:13). Before choosing the disciples He spent the night alone on a mountainside and prayed (Luke 6:12–16). And on the eve of His execution, He spent time alone in the Garden of Gethsemane, where He pondered the end of His life (Matt. 26:36). Reading these examples of Jesus, you might think, *Of course He prayed in solitude; He was God.* But we cannot escape the fact that in the midst of painful emotions, major decisions, and unthinkable circumstances, even Jesus needed to make space for His soul, allowing the Father to grasp Him.

Practically speaking, how do you go about practicing solitude and silence? If you are the type of person who needs a list of steps, you may be frustrated. The primary ingredients of Christian solitude and silence are this: doing nothing in the presence of God. The first time I spent a day alone in silence at a retreat center, I armed myself with my laptop, books, and planning calendar. I didn't understand that the point of this discipline was to do nothing at all. The idea of what George MacDonald called "sacred idleness" was foreign to me.

"Solitude and silence" means being still and listening. So many voices vie for your attention. Before you are able to listen to the voice of God, you will probably need to listen to the voice of your soul. Ask yourself, *What are those voices, and where are they coming from?* Envision your feelings and internal experiences speaking to you like characters in the Sunday comics by a callout bubble. What words would you put in the bubble? Give the turbulence and restlessness a voice. As you listen to your soul, what might it be saying to you?

I can tell you from experience that unless you schedule time for solitude, it likely won't happen. Open up your calendar right now and block out the space, ideally twenty minutes per day. We don't hesitate to schedule time to work out, spend time with friends, or pursue hobbies. Make regular times for being alone with God.

## DISCOVER YOUR INNER SANCTUARY

As you persist in the practice of solitude and silence, you will discover an inner sanctuary. If you're a follower of Christ, you are the dwelling place of God the Father, God the Son, and God the Holy Spirit.

- "We are the temple of the living God" (2 Cor. 6:16).
- "To them God has chosen to make known . . . the glorious riches of this mystery, which is Christ in you, the hope of glory" (Col. 1:27).
- "In him you too are being built together to become a dwelling in which God lives by his Spirit" (Eph. 2:22).

God dwells at the center of your being. You are His temple, and through Christ, the Father, Son, and Holy Spirit dwell in you.

In chapter 1, I described a beautiful, ornate cathedral decorated with majestic buttresses and stained glass. The Cathedral of the Immaculate Conception is a *physical* space, but the sanctuary within you is a *spiritual* place far more glorious than anything constructed by human hands. In the true dwelling place of God, the doors are never bolted and the lights are always left on just for you. We can only see it with the eyes of our hearts (Eph. 1:18) and the attitude of a child (Matt. 18:1–2).

In the introduction to Teresa of Avila's classic work *The Interior Castle*, one author describes this place beautifully: "No one else controls access to this perfect place. Give yourself your own unconditional permission to go there. Absolve yourself of missing the mark again and again. Believe the incredible truth that the Beloved has chosen for his dwelling place the core of your own being because that is the single most beautiful place in all of creation. Waste no time. Enter the center of your soul."[6]

Modern Christianity has all but lost an understanding of the inner sanctuary. God never intended our faith to be a mere intellectual pursuit. He intended to restore humanity's ability to walk with God. He calls us to walk with Him from an inward place. When we are disconnected from this place, this center, we gravitate toward anything nearby that gives us a false sense of being centered.

Brother Lawrence was a fifteenth-century monk, best known for his writings that we know as *The Practice of the Presence of God*.[7] He taught how to develop an awareness and attentiveness to God's presence, and peacefully call our minds back to God whenever something distracts us. For men living in the twenty-first century, our default setting is fixed on "the practice of the presence" of anything that comes across our radar screen. Now we need to learn to practice *His* presence.

I remember speaking with a man I'll call Mark about facing the emptiness. With great frustration he related his difficulty of being able to sit still, remain attentive, or simply be engaged and present when he attempted to spend time with God. I assured him that his frustrations were a common struggle. Then I asked him what seemed like a totally inappropriate question.

"What would it be like if during your time with God you were to imagine the hottest, most sexually appealing woman, and focus on her for twenty minutes? Would that change anything?"

Mark smiled impishly. "Well . . . yes, but that would be a sin."

In no way was I encouraging him to sin, or even attempt to do what I was asking. But my hypothetical question allowed our conversation to take an important turn. What we ended up discussing was that he *was able* to be still, attentive, engaged, and present. The only requirement was that he had to be looking at porn.

This was no small insight. With no awareness whatsoever that his brain had become wired for porn, or that he was addicted to his own brain chemistry, Mark had wrongly concluded that he just couldn't engage and be attentive because he was somehow deficient and unspiritual. Do you hear the lie even here? The lie he came to believe was that he didn't love God and must not care very deeply about the kingdom. As soon as he understood the basic way his brain worked, he was able to separate his brain rewiring from the novelty of porn from his true heart.

To sit in the presence of Divine Love is the single most transforming experience a person can have. But too many men I know have little ability or skill to do this. Yes, we were created for adventure, and we thrive when we are physically active. But I think it's something more than that. If we are ever going to learn to freely delight in God, we must first learn to be delighted in. It may not sound very "masculine" to you. But isn't this the point of all porn? It's not just the breasts and body parts; it's the woman in the image offering you her whole self because she *wants* you. The illusion, at least initially, is that *she* delights in *you*. He wants to touch and be touched, to see and be seen. One of the main reasons why we find it so easy to sit with rapt attention, transfixed upon the counterfeit love of porn, is that it "delights" in us.

"We love because he first loved us," wrote John (1 John 4:19). Right now, in the core of your being, do you actually believe, sense, know, and feel that your heavenly Father delights in you? If not, imagine what it might be like to sit in His presence, with no other goal except to be delighted in.

## DISCOVER PRAYER THAT CENTERS YOUR SOUL

Ten years ago I decided that I no longer wanted to live off of other people's spirituality. I no longer wanted to settle for hearing about other people's encounters with God, and only teach others what I could glean from the books I was reading. I wanted to experience God as David did. I wanted to dwell in the sanctuary of God and "gaze on the beauty of the LORD and . . . seek him in his temple" (Ps. 27:4). But honestly, I had no idea how to do this without performing the familiar routine of trying harder. About that time a respected colleague introduced me to contemplative prayer, and through it, I discovered that with God, less is more.

For centuries Christians have practiced a form of prayer that utters no words and focuses on attentiveness to the presence of God within. In modern times people have identified this type of prayer by several names: *centering prayer, contemplative prayer,* or *meditative prayer*. But all of these practices are basically the same. Centering prayer allows for an intimacy that is deeper than words can express. As you practice this prayer of stillness and attentiveness, the gospel will come alive to you experientially. For the rest of the chapter, I will focus on centering prayer, since this is how I have developed my prayer life in the last several years.

Centering prayer helps us find our spiritual and emotional

center and increases our faith. As we experience His loving presence, our walk with God becomes less and less dependent upon what we intellectually believe, and more dependent upon what we have tasted, seen, and heard. We experience His delight in us. His fragrance becomes real. As we grow increasingly acclimated to contemplative prayer, we find that faith, hope, and love begin to replace our unbelief, idolatry, and self-concern. I can't think of another premodern practice so relevant to the postmodern struggle with porn.

People steeped in the contemplative life suggest that you spend no fewer than twenty minutes per day in centering prayer. A number of my friends engage in centering prayer for twenty minutes in the morning and twenty minutes in the evening. From a pragmatic perspective, their reports have been astonishing. They describe an increase in concentration, attention span, mood regulation, and self-control. They feel much more connected to their hearts and are living more deeply from the center of their beings, where Jesus dwells.

An excellent resource for beginning the practice of contemplative prayer is J. David Muyskens's book *Forty Days to a Closer Walk with God*.[8] Not only does the book include guidelines and background for learning centering prayer but also it is divided into forty brief writings that will guide you from day to day. For the man who is rebooting and rewiring himself from sexual compulsion to sexual sobriety, it provides a simple structure to direct your focus and attention away from porn.

In his book, Muyskens listed four simple guidelines for centering prayer.

1. *Choose a sacred word as a symbol of your desire to be present to God.*

    When you think of God, what word comes to mind? When you pray to Him, what do you call Him? Lord? Savior? Father? When I think of God, the first word that comes to my mind is *Abba*—Aramaic for "Papa" (Mark 14:36). The word that most easily comes to mind when you think of God is the best place to start.

2. *Sit comfortably in a quiet place.*

Make sure you are sitting somewhere comfortable in an environment that is free from internal and external distractions. The noise around you and within you will seem amplified as you begin to quiet yourself. The point of centering prayer is not to block out distractions and empty your mind until you're left with a blank slate. You don't get more points for being less distracted. The goal in centering prayer is to be present to yourself and present to God.

3. *When interrupted by thoughts, sounds, or other distractions, acknowledge them and gently return your attention to God via the sacred word.*

If a random thought or distraction interferes, let it go. As soon as you become aware that you are distracted, simply return to your sacred word that in turn refocuses your awareness of God's presence.

4. *At the end of the prayer period, remain in silence with your eyes closed for several minutes.*

When finished, keep your eyes closed so you don't jar yourself back to your surroundings. Ideally, after centering prayer, you'll want to stay in that centered space for a little while.

## CAN ANCIENT PRAYER REWIRE YOUR BRAIN?

*Okay, Michael. This all sounds hopeful. But will solitude and silence, centering prayer, and inward attentiveness really make a difference in my struggle with porn?* That's a very important question. The scientific verdict is in, and the answer is a *qualified* yes.

Although no scientific studies deal explicitly with centering prayer, significant evidence connects the practice of mindfulness meditation[9] with recovery from addiction, compulsive behaviors, and other psychological disorders.[10] In a definitive study, Alan Marlatt, from the University of Washington's Addictive Behavior Research Center, found evidence that meditation-based spiritual interventions were strongly associated with reduced alcohol and substance use.[11]

If you remember from chapter 10, two necessary factors involved in neurological rewiring are *attention* and *focus*. Countless scientific studies have demonstrated that our brains are wired according to what we give our attention and focus to—*what fires together, wires together*.[12] Centering prayer involves simultaneously giving intentional focus and sustained attention to our inner world and our triune God.

But there's more. Centering prayer, like the secular practice of mindfulness, teaches that thoughts, feelings, and sensations should be accepted and acknowledged without judgment. This is important for two reasons. First, fighting cravings and urges generally leads to increased craving. It's the classic *Don't think about a pink elephant.* Second, acknowledging our thoughts and feelings, while remaining focused on and attentive to God's presence, allows us to gain awareness of our urges, cravings, and triggers.

In the next chapter we will look closely at how you can apply centering prayer to the everyday care of your soul.

12

# The Soul Care Highway

Life is shaped by the end you live for. You are
made in the image of what you desire.

**—THOMAS MERTON**

The pancake house was about to close when the real conversation began. The moment my friend Connor said, "We've known each other for almost fifteen years, and there's something I need to tell you," I knew we were done with the small talk. Earlier in the day Connor had called and asked to meet for coffee after the kids were in bed. My hunch was right. He didn't want to talk about football.

Our friendship had never ventured below surface issues, so this was the first time he shared about what was really going on inside his soul. Knowing my story, he courageously decided to risk letting me see beneath his mask of control as he poured out his heart. Nothing shocked me as he described his lifelong struggle with lust, masturbation, and pornography. I'll never forget the lifeless look of shame that covered him from head to toe. Connor was done with the game-playing and lying to himself. He was tired of being two different men.

"I'm ready to deal with this," he said. "I want to be whole."

## THE SOUL CARE HIGHWAY IS
## YOUR PATH TO FREEDOM

Walking with Connor and watching his transformation has been one of my greatest joys. As if a dimmer switch in the depths of his being had been turned from its darkest setting to "high beam," the light in his soul grew from a flicker to full brightness. For several years now we have walked together as two broken men discovering what it means to follow Jesus on a path where He makes our broken hearts whole. Along the way, God has given us the privilege of walking with other men who have come to know deep restoration. My fervent prayer and singular hope is that you will join us on the journey.

This chapter offers my best description of the journey we have taken. It isn't a detailed set of directions, like a GPS that tells you when to turn and how far until you reach your destination. It functions more as an atlas that gives you a general lay of the land and what you need to know to get from point to point. Though the following diagram implies a neat and tidy progression from one stage to the next, it is by no means a linear process. All true spirituality is messy spirituality. We take wrong turns. We get lost. We don't stop and ask for directions. But as God restores our souls, He faithfully guides us in paths of righteousness (Ps. 23:3).

"How blessed is the man whose strength is in You, in whose heart are the highways to Zion," the psalmist wrote (84:5 NASB). When you surrendered your life to Christ, He not only gave you a new heart but He set the compass to true north and pointed you in the right direction to Zion, the city of God. Knowing that you have a highway in your heart should be very comforting. You may get disoriented and lose your way, but you can always return to the highway. It's right there in your heart.

In chapter 7 I described the soul snare cycle as a downward spiral of addiction, compulsion, and idolatry. In that chapter I also shared the first part of Proverbs 22:5: "In the paths of the wicked lie thorns and snares . . ." I did not share, however, the second part of the verse, "but he who guards his soul stays far from them." If we want to live free of addictive snares, we need to guard our souls. That doesn't mean we protect them from the pain of a broken world. It means we are proactive, attentive, and alert about the life within.

Because our souls are of inestimable value to God—purchased with the blood of Christ—we need to pay attention to them, care for them, nurture the life within them, and defend them against attack. We also need to guard our souls because they are the dwelling place of God. The Soul Care Highway illustration that follows will help you experience care and transformation for your soul.

## The Soul Care Highway

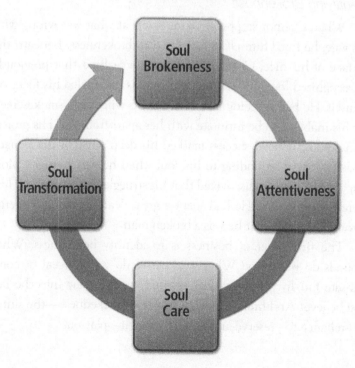

# SOUL BROKENNESS: IT CAN BE TRANSFORMED

When Connor first shared his struggle with me, he felt guilty and knew his porn habit was eroding his heart and marriage. In many of our initial conversations, he kept pointing the finger at his wife. She was not cooperative in bed like he wanted. She didn't understand his sexual needs. Her desires were incompatible with his. She had medical issues throughout their marriage that made things more complex than he wanted. In short, he insisted that if she decided to change in order to meet his needs, then he would be able to rein in his sexual desires. Everyone else needed to get fixed, not him.

## Identifying Brokenness

When Connor stopped looking solely at what was wrong with his wife, he freed himself to face his own brokenness. Beneath the surface of his nice, Christian persona, he realized that previously unrecognized longings and angry demands had fueled his focus on himself. He began seeing that blaming his wife was a smokescreen for his inability to be intimate with her apart from sex. His professional and financial success masked his deep sense of inadequacy and significant wounding to his soul when he was younger. Most important, Connor discovered that his struggles with porn and lust were not about sex. He had spent a great deal of time and energy covering the fact that he was a broken man.

The first order of business is to identify brokenness. What wounds do you carry? What weaknesses do you conceal or compensate for? In what way does spiritual warfare play into the lies you believe? And finally, in what way does wickedness—the sinful self-reliance to preserve and protect yourself—play out?

*Making the Connection Between Brokenness and Porn*

Another mile marker on the highway to soul transformation is assessing the broken promises porn has made to you. Remember "The Broken Promises of Porn" from chapter 2? Does porn promise

- to validate your manhood without requiring strength?
- sexual fulfillment without relationship?
- intimacy without risk and suffering?
- passion and life without connection to your soul?
- power over women, without responsibility?
- comfort and care without needing to depend on others?

Jesus came to bind up the brokenhearted and set captives free. Though not every wound can be fully healed this side of heaven, there is substantial healing available in Christ. Far more healing is available for our souls than we would ever believe. And so we bring our hearts, our wounds, to God, and we seek healing. We begin this process by learning to be attentive.

## SOUL ATTENTIVENESS: IT CAN BE DEVELOPED

The next stop on the soul care highway is *soul attentiveness*. Soul attentiveness means being observant and aware of your inner world. It is neither morbid introspection nor paralyzing analysis. In the Psalms we see David, the man after God's own heart, practicing soul attentiveness. As a warrior king–poet, he neither lived with the superficial air that *It's all good* nor was inwardly cut off or self-absorbed. David was keenly attentive to his inner world. His heartfelt reflections in the Psalms reflect this. Other men contributed their deepest reflections to the Psalms as well.

Years ago, many of us sang a chorus in church based on Psalm 42:1. The song goes, "As the deer panteth for the water, so my soul longeth after thee . . ."[1] We never really paid attention to the fact that the psalmist was basically saying, "As a dehydrated, dying animal seeks water, so does my parched soul." The psalmist, whom Scripture describes as a son of Korah, was not painting a pretty picture here. Psalm 42 is a song of lament that reflects his grief over the loss of his community.

As the psalmist pours out his heart to God, he seems to stop dead in his tracks to ask a question. "Why are you downcast, O my soul? Why so disturbed within me?" (Ps. 42:5). Then he pours out his heart again, pauses, and repeats the same question. "Why are you downcast, O my soul? Why so disturbed within me?" (v. 11; see also 43:5). Notice that the psalmist is engaged in a conversation with God, but he is also engaged in a conversation with himself as the basis for his dialogue with God. It's a beautiful picture of a man being attentive to his soul.

## FOUR WAYS TO PRACTICE SOUL ATTENTIVENESS

As I reflect back on my sexual addiction, I often wonder how my life would have been different if I'd had a language at my disposal to help me understand what was going on in my soul. As I work with men today, whenever possible, I try to help them develop a soul language. Four related actions will help you develop your own soul language.

### Stalk Your Triggers

You may recall from chapter 7 that triggers are cues that reflexively elicit cravings and urges to act out sexually. Identifying what places, people, circumstances, or experiences trip your trigger is key.

What provokes lust, craving, and movement toward porn? No trigger is insignificant if it serves as a cue to lust and craving. I know a man for whom a certain perfume triggers him. Another man was triggered by women with auburn hair.

Many men find it helpful to make a list of triggers. As you do this, try to picture your triggers as stealth operatives strategically positioned on a battlefield. In your moments of vulnerability, those operatives launch into full assault. Your job is to stalk them and learn their positions so you can shut them down.

### Interrogate Your Cravings

Imagine a prisoner of war nervously sitting in an interrogation room. A single lightbulb hangs over his head as the examiner demands that the prisoner reveal everything he knows. Now imagine that you are that examiner, and that the prisoner is your uncontrollable craving. Sound strange? Actually, if your cravings could tell you everything they knew, you might be surprised. On one level the phenomenon of craving is part of your physical, biological makeup.

On another level, your cravings *do* talk to you. They are the physiological expressions of thirst and longing, communicating to you that a legitimate desire is not being met. What is the craving about? What is the longing beneath the urge? What is the legitimate desire? Before learning to interrogate their cravings, I hear men say, "I'm just really horny." But after learning this method of soul attentiveness, men say, "I'm not horny; beneath feeling sexually aroused, what I really feel is lonely."

### Surf Your Urges

By now you probably understand that white-knuckling and gritting your teeth is not going to take you to the root of your lust issue. Sure, at times you need to exert your will and resist temptation, but if you only suppress them, your urges and cravings will come back to you with even greater ferocity. One way of dealing with these is to practice *urge surfing.*

Addiction researcher Alan Marlatt, from the University of Washington, coined the term *urge surfing* by comparing addictive cravings to ocean waves. Cravings, like waves, start small, gain momentum, and eventually dissipate. In fact, the most intense cravings and urges rarely last more than thirty minutes. If you try to swim through a decent-sized wave in the ocean, you will be drawn under the water no matter how hard you resist. However, if you turn and ride the wave as it passes by, you will be able to continue your swim. Urge surfing is similar. Rather than fight cravings directly, you can consciously acknowledge the urges and ride them out until they pass. This can be especially helpful during the process of rebooting and rewiring your brain.

Here's an example of what urge surfing might look like with porn or lust. Say you are home alone and haven't looked at porn for two weeks. Suddenly, you start thinking about going online and surfing for porn. The first step is simply to *observe.* Sit comfortably in a chair and take a few deep breaths to help you get centered. Then take an inventory across your body. Where is the urge coming from in your body? Where do you feel it? Is it a feeling in your gut, shoulders, genitals? What is the sensation? Is it emptiness? Is it tingling? Anxiety? Now comes the part that requires a little courage. Speak out loud what you are experiencing: "I'm feeling a craving . . . it feels like butterflies in my stomach. It's a light, hollow sensation." Say whatever you are experiencing three or four times out loud.

Now that you have observed what the craving is, the next step is to *focus.* Direct your focus on one specific area where you are experiencing the urge. Notice the exact sensations. Focus on the lightness, or hollowness, or tension. Observe how large of an area the sensation takes up. Is it the size of a baseball? Or is it the size of a pinprick? As you focus upon the sensation, describe it to yourself out loud. For example, "My heart rate seems faster. I can feel my face flush. I feel an energy in my temples." As an outside observer of yourself, keep noticing the sensations and experiences and describe them out loud.

The third step is to *refocus*. Return again to each part of your body where you experience the urge or craving. Are you able to observe any sensory changes? You may perceive after several minutes of urge surfing that the cravings have decreased or altogether disappeared. It's important to say here that the point of urge surfing is not to eliminate cravings, but to experience them differently. Instead of running into the wave of craving, you are riding on top of it. Knowing that you can ride even the biggest wave is empowering. In the early stage of recovery, you can practice this until you are so familiar with the urges that they no longer trouble you.

## Carry Your Tension

In his book *The Holy Longing*, Catholic priest and seminary president Ronald Rolheiser tells a story from a class he attended in graduate school.[2] One day, as his professor was lecturing on sexuality and morality, the issue of masturbation was raised. A student stopped the professor dead in his tracks with an audacious question: Do you masturbate? The professor's immediate reaction was anger at the student's blatant disrespect. He turned away from the class, faced the blackboard, and was silent. After he composed himself he turned and addressed the student:

"My first reaction is to tell you that you're out of order and that you've no business asking a question like that in this class, or anywhere else. However, since this is a class in moral theology and in the end your question has some value, I will in fact answer you: Yes, sometimes I do—and I'm not proud of it. I don't think it's very wrong and I don't think it's very right either. I do know this though . . . I'm a better person when I don't because then I am carrying more of the tension that we, all of us, should carry in this life. I'm a better person when I carry that tension."

Carrying tension in this way is not an ascetic act of self-denial; it is an act of love. More often than not, when men masturbate, they cut off or detach from their souls. After the immediate ecstasy and release of tension, they experience a weakened sense of strength for having spent themselves. This occurs not only on the physical level, but on the emotional and spiritual level as well.

Of the hundreds of men I've counseled about their sexual addictions, not one has told me that after masturbating he felt stronger, more confident, and more vitally connected to the deep part of his soul. Debates over whether or not masturbation is a sin totally miss the point. The crucial question is not whether masturbation is right or wrong. The question is, as it is with any thought or behavior, does it hinder our spiritual, emotional, and social maturity? Does it stand in the way of love?

So what does it mean to carry the tension? In physics, tension is defined as the *magnitude of pulling force* exerted by another object. Carrying tension begins by recognizing that a force is pulling against you, toward the path of least resistance. This force seeks the easiest resolution for the least amount of effort. It is a force pulling for the diminishment of your soul.

The other force, I believe, is the image of God within you—the *imago dei*. This force is heroic, and its magnitude is immeasurable. It compels firefighters to run back into the flames and soldiers to run back through enemy fire to save their comrades. More commonly, it displays itself in the tender strength of a husband who moves toward his wife when she is angry. It reveals itself in the courage of a terrified young man asking a girl to the homecoming dance. It is the gospel reality behind all spiritual growth—when we lose our lives we find them (Luke 9:24).

Carrying tension always involves necessary suffering and embracing our pain, not because we are masochistic, but because the pain leads to well-being and growth of our souls. Like our physical muscles that grow when stretched to the limit, the muscles of our souls grow when we carry the tension.

## SOUL CARE: WHAT YOUR SOUL NEEDS NOW

Next, we reach the stage appropriately titled *soul care*. Soul care brings together your interior life with the rest of your life. This is how God created you to live, as an integrated whole person. Soul care promotes the restoration and well-being of your soul so your spiritual, emotional, relational, and physical parts benefit as well. Discussing these dimensions as separate entities can be misleading since they interrelate with the others. What happens in a given dimension has an impact on every other dimension.

In teaching men to practice soul care, I encourage them to focus on two questions: The first is, *What does my soul really need right now?* Remember, porn and lust mask your real needs. Every man experiences needs related to what's happening in the here and now. Being hungry or tired, for example. Short-term and long-term needs must also be considered. What is a healthy amount of hours to work? What would your ideal week look like with God? With friends and family? What are those real needs?

The second question is, *How can I begin to meet those needs in a legitimate, healthy way?* For Connor this was significant. As he realized that sexual intercourse had become a substitute for emotional and spiritual intimacy with his wife, he made it a point to regularly pursue nonsexual physical affection, which became a blessing to both of them. She didn't feel so much pressure, which in turn helped her feel a greater freedom to give herself to her husband, emotionally, physically, spiritually, and sexually. He felt more emotionally and spiritually connected to his wife and discovered that his demand for sex decreased.

### What Does the Physical "You" Need?

What does it mean to care for who you are as a physical being? How would you describe your energy level? What are your eating habits? Do you exercise? How do you manage the physical side of tension and stress? Do you have sleep issues? When was the last time you had a complete physical? Each of these issues can be related to emotional and relational health as well. When you are not well physically, it affects every other aspect of your life.

### What Does the Relational "You" Need?

When a man is preoccupied with a sexual compulsion like porn, relationships and social interactions tend to suffer. Sexual compulsions are disorders of intimacy. By definition, they lead to isolation and loneliness—even if a man is addicted to relationships. When relational needs are neglected, porn becomes an easy substitute.

### What Does the Emotional "You" Need?

One of the most thoughtful books I've read in the last few years is Peter Scazzero's *Emotionally Healthy Spirituality*.[3] One of his main points is that we cannot separate our emotional health from our spiritual health. You can take a free emotional health assessment at www.emotionallyhealthy.org.

### What Does the Spiritual "You" Need?

As discussed in chapter 11, one of our greatest spiritual needs is solitude/silence. In those times alone ask yourself what your ideal spiritual "you" would look like. Then ask God what He wants to say to you.

## SOUL TRANSFORMATION

A tremendous amount of courage is required to break through the counterfeit pleasures of porn and face the realities of your own heart. Today my friend Connor would tell you that this confrontation has been one of the hardest and most painful chapters of his life. But he would also say that this has been the most fruitful season of his life. He and his wife enjoy a marriage that is richer, deeper, and more real than he ever imagined possible.

So what happened to his inferno of lust and struggle with porn? Today, it occasionally flickers, reminding him that his sexuality is not so much something to be suppressed and managed but rather understood as a window into his soul. That flicker acts like the warning light on a car dashboard. It's there, and it comes on when something below the hood needs attention.

On this side of heaven, transformed souls don't exist, only souls that are in the process of transforming. We should never measure transformation by the absence of sin, only by the presence of love, joy, peace, patience, kindness, goodness, faithfulness, gentleness, and self-control (Gal. 5:22–23). In addition to losing the compulsion toward lust and porn, several other signs will tell you that the Spirit of God is transforming your life. Be attentive for an ever-increasing presence of faith, hope, and love. *Faith* is the conviction that God really is who He says He is. Trustworthy. Good. Sufficient. *Hope* is placing your heart's desires and longings in His hands. *Love* is the overflow of a heart that is full from love.

Your journey down the soul care highway may have begun long ago or it may be just beginning. Either way, the path that lies ahead needs more exploration. Let's unpack this in the next chapter.

# Freedom to Live

The biggest human temptation is to settle for too little.

**—THOMAS MERTON**

"Timmy, when was the last time you saw Eddie?" I asked with an edge of tension in my voice.

"Not since the third inning—when he went to get a hot dog," answered Timmy.

The seventh-inning stretch had just concluded with the Cleveland Indians playing to a packed house. I was a youth minister at the time, and I was hanging out with two teenage brothers whose dad died unexpectedly two years earlier. Timmy was the quiet, compliant brother, while Eddie, three years older, was the wild, rebellious one. His rapidly growing police record was becoming legend in his neighborhood. I was bound and determined that under my watch, this would be an uneventful outing.

As the players returned to the field and the fans started sitting down, a commotion broke out near third base. An unruly fan had jumped on to the field and was running straight across the outfield toward the right field foul pole. I will never forget what happened next: the fan dropped his pants in center field.

While the fan exposed his back side, the crowd of over fifty thousand people jumped back to their feet and went wild. Several police officers, long past their prime, joined in hot pursuit across the outfield. That's when the entertainment began. After pulling up his pants, the fan—who apparently failed to think through his strategy of escape—zig-zagged through the cops in a game of cat and mouse.

Then I realized the fan was Eddie. Earlier, he had run into a friend who offered him twenty bucks to bare his bottom in center field. As the police squeezed in on him, Eddie ran to right field and jumped the fence, into the arms of security where he was promptly handcuffed.

To the best of my recollection, I don't ever remember attending a youth ministry seminar about what to do when one of your youth group kids commits an act of indecent exposure in front of fifty thousand people.

That day gave me a whole new understanding of the biblical idea of being naked and unashamed. On an obvious level, Eddie was naked *and* unashamed. But Eddie's foolish act exposed something in me. I felt so out of control. Deeper than that, I felt ashamed. Foolish. Like a failure. I imagined what others would be saying. *Why wasn't I keeping an eye on him?* I asked myself. *How did this happen? And if this occurred under my watch, maybe Eddie doesn't respect me.*

As a youth minister, I had developed a reputation for working with nice kids. Compliant kids. Kids who never threatened my sense of adequacy or control. But there I was, twenty years old, feeling pretty inadequate. I felt out of control and didn't like it. It was a form of nakedness that I was unaccustomed to.

## THE FREEDOM OF BEING OUR NAKED SELVES

All of us experience moments in our lives where we either get caught with our pants down or are exposed in a moment of inadequacy. In the process, our naked selves are revealed. One's naked self is the self that is hidden and alone. Wicked, wounded, and weak, broken and impoverished. It holds no charm, credential, accomplishment, or status. Henri Nouwen called it the "irrelevant self."[1] It is the self that, apart from God's loving pursuit, we try to conceal. In order to *be* ourselves, we each must come to terms with our naked selves.

On the night He was betrayed, Jesus shared a meal with His disciples. At the end of the meal, He stood up from the table and gave us an extraordinary picture of God's love. Like a common house servant, Jesus wrapped a towel around *His* waist, poured water into a basin, and began to wash the dirty, road-worn feet of His disciples. Among those feet were Judas's and Peter's. One man would betray Him; the other would deny Him—before the night was over (John 13:1–8). Still, Jesus knelt down before them.

Today, God's love kneels down to us, wherever we are. And as He does, He urges us to bare our selves before Him. Why? Because in seeing our naked selves in the light of God's love, we make two discoveries. First, we discover more clearly who *God* is. All of the brokenness in our world and in our lives calls into question God's goodness. Can we trust Him? Is He really enough? In our nakedness, there is no pretense of earning or obtaining His love. It's a gift that makes the gospel more real.

Only in our nakedness can we experience the Father's mercy, tenderness, and healing and realize that we are neither shamed nor despised. In this place we know in our hearts that our poverty and brokenness are the currency of heaven by which we can obtain all the riches that are stocked on the shelves of God's abundant storehouses.

If the first discovery we make in our nakedness is who God is, the second discovery is who *we* are. As we realize that we are loved beyond imagination, we discover that this alone defines our true identities. We are the beloved. Because of this, we are free from the compulsion to be someone we are not—to impress, manipulate, or attempt in our own unique way to earn love. We are free to be who we are.

## TRUE FREEDOM MEANS MOVING TOWARD GOD'S HEART

These two discoveries bring us freedom. But what is freedom?

In the American South before the Civil War, slaves were owned by someone. The owner determined where his slaves could go, what they could do, and what their day-to-day lives looked like. The master totally controlled the slave.

At the conclusion of the Civil War in 1865, all slaves in the South were emancipated. But emancipation meant much more than freeing slaves from a plantation or oppressive labor. It was also a declaration that every former slave was considered a full person, with the right to direct the course of his own life as he pleased. According to the rule of the land, all people—including the former slaves—were granted the right to be treated with the dignity of a person made in God's image.

Freedom is like a coin. Breaking free from the chains of porn is only one side of the coin. Both sides, however, offer the complete picture. Freedom is not just *from* something (the first side of the coin); it also is freedom *toward* something (the other side)—the ability to do what you most deeply want to, and to become who you most deeply are.

As you embrace this freedom, you can begin to direct your will according to your truest desires. You can make healthy choices and exercise self-control. *You* decide whether or not you will stare at a woman's breasts, masturbate to porn, have sex with your girlfriend, or flirt with the woman at your office. This is what the Bible means by *self-control*.

One day, while sitting in a Starbucks coffee shop, I came across a friend I hadn't seen in a few years. As we spent several minutes catching each other up on our lives, he made it a point to let me know that his struggle with porn was largely a thing of the past.

"What took me by surprise," he said, "was that once my porn habit was broken, God really started working on some deep issues in my heart." His words reminded me of George Carlin's famous line: "Just 'cause you got the monkey off your back doesn't mean the circus has left town."

My friend's comment didn't surprise me, though, because our heavenly Father desires to give us fullness, abundance, and freedom. And in order for us to receive them, He must make room for them in our hearts by working on our deeper issues.

God is concerned with so much more than giving you the energy to keep you from looking at porn. Obviously, He wants you free from any bondage—including porn and lust—that stands in the way of your relationship with Him. But in the big picture, He wants to free you from any encumbrances (related or unrelated to porn) that prevent you from living the life He intended. Remember, David wrote that he ran in the path of God's commands (Ps. 119:32) because his heart had been set free. So what does this life of freedom—the life God intended for all of us—look like?

## GOD WANTS TO TRANSFORM YOU INTO AN OAK OF RIGHTEOUSNESS

In His first public sermon, Jesus described His reason for leaving His Father in heaven to live among us. Luke tells us that after Jesus fasted and prayed in the desert for forty days, being tempted by the devil, He began His public ministry. Full of the Holy Spirit, Jesus returned to His hometown of Galilee. On the Sabbath day, He walked into the synagogue where people had gathered for worship and picked up a scroll. It's important to point out that the scroll in His hands did not come from an Old Testament grab bag nor did He randomly pluck a verse for the day out of thin air. The words Jesus read appeared in the Hebrew liturgical calendar—specific readings that were predetermined long before He set foot in the temple. He unrolled the scroll and read:

> *The Spirit of the Lord is on me,*
> > *because he has anointed me*
> > *to preach good news to the poor.*
> *He has sent me to proclaim freedom for the prisoners*
> > *and recovery of sight for the blind,*
> *to release the oppressed,*
> > *to proclaim the year of the Lord's favor. (Luke 4:18–19)*

These words, taken from Isaiah 61, describe the benefits of enjoying a living relationship with Jesus Christ. It's a gospel of restoration. A gospel of healing. A gospel of transformation where people hear good news, give their lives to Christ, receive healing and wholeness for their hearts, and experience freedom from the pain of living in a broken world. Jesus offers this to us so that we might know Him and make Him known.

Haven't we all heard political candidates declare who they are, what they stand for, and what they promise to do if elected? Similarly, this was Jesus' very first public sermon; He was letting everyone know what He stood for and what He was all about. As Jesus read the first few verses of Isaiah 61, He promised to take all that is broken and bring glory out of it.

Isaiah 61 further describes the ministry of the coming Messiah, presumably Jesus. We don't know if Jesus quoted the next part of Isaiah or not while He spoke in the synagogue, but it certainly sounds like Jesus. The book of Isaiah says that the Spirit of the Lord anointed Jesus for these reasons:

> *to comfort all who mourn,*
> *and provide for those who grieve in Zion—*
> *to bestow on them a crown of beauty*
>     *instead of ashes,*
> *the oil of gladness*
>     *instead of mourning,*
> *and a garment of praise*
>     *instead of a spirit of despair.* (61:2–3)

Finally, at the end of verse 3, Isaiah wrote of the beneficiaries of Jesus' ministry:

> *They will be called oaks of righteousness,*
>     *a planting of the* LORD
>     *for the display of his splendor.*

Isaiah said that because of Jesus' healing work in our lives, we will be called "oaks of righteousness." Today, "oaks" might stir up images of wood furniture or autumn calendars. But if you had lived in Isaiah's or Jesus' day, you would have known that this was a stunning promise. You see, in ancient times, people worshipped and offered sacrifices to their pagan gods in groves of oak trees. Earlier in Isaiah, God addressed these practices:

> *You will be ashamed because of the sacred oaks*
>     *in which you have delighted;*
> *you will be disgraced because of the gardens*
>     *that you have chosen.*

*You will be like an oak with fading leaves,*
  *like a garden without water.*
*The mighty man will become tinder*
  *and his work a spark;*
*both will burn together,*
  *with no one to quench the fire. (1:29–31)*

In rebellion, God's people had forsaken Him to gather in secretive oak groves and worship the pagan gods of the ancient cultures around them—gods with names like Baal, Asherah, and Molech.

In our contemporary world of religious tolerance and diversity, we might be tempted to sanitize this scene. But the people in Isaiah's day knew otherwise; they knew these gods required their followers to engage in a wide variety of promiscuous, truly pornographic sexual practices outside of God's design—orgies, adultery, prostitution, even the bloody human sacrifice of children—all in the name of "worship." They were practicing both physical and spiritual infidelity.

In Isaiah 57, God connects the dots between idolatry and adultery—both of which occurred under the "oaks":

*You burn with lust among the oaks*
  *and under every spreading tree;*
*you sacrifice your children in the ravines*
  *and under the overhanging crags.*
*The idols among the smooth stones of the ravines are your portion;*
  *they, they are your lot.*
*Yes, to them you have poured out drink offerings*
  *and offered grain offerings.*
  *In the light of these things, should I relent?*
*You have made your bed on a high and lofty hill;*
  *there you went up to offer your sacrifices. (vv. 5–7)*

And then in verse 8 Isaiah wrote:

> *Behind your doors and your doorposts*
> *you have put your pagan symbols.*
> *Forsaking me, you uncovered your bed,*
> *you climbed into it and opened it wide;*
> *you made a pact with those whose beds you love,*
> *and you looked with lust on their naked bodies.* (UPDATED NIV)

Here is a graphic picture of God's chosen people intentionally worshipping foreign gods. This is not an image of an Israelite who just happened to walk down the road and got pulled into a pagan temple. This is a picture of God's chosen people giving themselves over to these foreign gods—heart, soul, and body. As part of the regular practice of worshipping these gods, people placed symbols throughout their homes in the same way that today we might hang a cross on the wall or affix a fish bumper sticker on the back of our car.

So what did these pagan symbols look like? They were usually highly sexual. For instance, the goddess Asherah (known elsewhere as Aphrodite) was the goddess of fertility. So it's no wonder that the symbol identifying her was the phallus. When the Old Testament refers to God's chosen people worshipping at the Asherah "poles," it is actually talking about the Jews gathering around and performing pagan religious rituals around a tall tower or temple built in the shape of a man's genitalia.

Contrary to popular opinion, worship like this did not die out centuries ago. While on a ministry trip to Southeast Asia, I witnessed these symbols firsthand, both in the streets, as monuments, and in the community, on buildings. One of my most surprising encounters with an Asherah pole occurred in one of the larger retail stores, where a very large section was dedicated to rows and rows of wooden phallic symbols. Some were several feet high and some were inches high. Some were made to hang on the wall, the rearview mirror, or a keychain. Others were medallions or photographs. Each amulet stood for generative power, blessing, and fertility.

In the United States, you'd need to go to an adult bookstore or novelty shop to find anything that competes with these mass-marketed phallic idols. Regardless of where we find them, the symbolism and idolatry of Asherah's oaks transcend biblical times. Clearly God is saying that the oaks were often traditional places of *unrighteousness*—especially sexual sin and immorality.

So now, returning to Isaiah 61 and reading God's offer to make our hearts whole, set us free, and make us *oaks of righteousness* who will display His glory, we gain a whole new understanding. In the very place of sin and shame and failure, the very places where we need to seek God's help and healing, He promises to make us oaks of righteousness.

That secret, hidden place of your greatest struggle, failure, or shame? That's exactly where God wants to meet you. I should know. It happened to me. But most men struggling with porn feel like anything but an oak of righteousness. They have been fighting a losing battle or just giving in. They have resigned themselves to battling, struggling with cycles of defeat, believing deep down that this is as good as it gets.

This is *not* as good as it gets. The gospel offers us another way, but practically speaking, where do you begin? Right back to the soul care path. Deep transformation is possible; in fact, it is your birthright, but no quick fix is available.

The invitation to lasting freedom seems at best idealistic, and at worst a cruel invitation to hope. But in reality, God passionately desires to transform you from a twig of shame—think Charlie Brown's Christmas tree—into an oak of righteousness that will display His splendor, His glory—like one of the mighty redwood trees in Yosemite.

# SELLING EVERYTHING TO
# BUY THE TREASURE

I've always been drawn to the story in the gospel of Matthew where a man finds buried treasure in a field, sells everything he has, then buys the field (13:44). Throughout the years of my addiction, I identified with the man in Jesus' parable, except I had sold everything for porn. But the passion, risk, and singular purpose of the man in the story kept something alive in me.

Nearly three decades ago, while attending a Young Life leadership camp in upstate New York, I prayed a prayer that haunts me to this day. At the end of the final training session, the speaker sent us into the chilly night air to spend twenty minutes alone with God. The theme for three days had been "positioning our lives for the greatest possible kingdom impact." I'll never forget how difficult it was to sit for twenty minutes in silence. In addition to feeling empty and anxious, all I could think about were all my shortcomings, failures, and reasons why I would probably never have an impact on the kingdom of God.

I also recall hearing the distant echo beneath the accusing voices, encouraging me to live my life well for the kingdom of God. Now I know it was my good heart, but then I didn't know how this would happen or even if it could happen in light of my secret struggles. But the desire was unmistakable.

At the end of twenty minutes, a bell rang to signify that our time was up. Walking back to my room, I bumped into my friend Peter. As we shared, I discovered that the same passion was stirring inside of him. We both felt as if something significant was happening, so we decided to pray together.

There, at the edge of Saranac Lake, we got down on our knees and prayed from our guts. My prayer went something this:

"Father, in Jesus You have given me life, forgiveness, and

cleansing. My deepest desire is to serve You and Your kingdom in whatever I do. But I know there's a whole bunch of crap that stands in the way. I long to be powerful in Your kingdom and strong for what You want to accomplish in me and through me. I want to know You, God. I want to know You more, walk more in Your ways, and live according to Your truth. I ask You to do *whatever it takes* in whatever part of my life, to use me as fully as possible. If anything whatsoever stands in the way of me knowing You, I give You permission to remove it, and I ask You to remove it. Please, God, *do whatever it takes*. I want to know You."

Years later, when my friend Eric knelt beside me in my closet, I began a prayer that I have prayed many times. I asked, "Jesus, what do You want to say to me?" What I heard was this: *Michael, do you remember the time at Saranac when you asked Me to do whatever it takes so that you could know Me more deeply? Do you remember when you gave Me permission to remove anything in your life that stands in the way of you knowing Me? That is what I have been doing. I love you so deeply that I will go to any expense to make you whole. It has taken you over twenty years to see it, but I am answering your prayer.*

And then it hit me. He had answered my prayer from years earlier. He was doing whatever it took.

Doing whatever it takes is not about proving yourself, trying harder, or ratcheting up your effort. God forbid. Wendell Berry wrote, "We can start from where we are, with what we have, and imagine and work for the healings that are necessary. But we must begin by giving up any idea that we can bring about these healings without fundamental changes in the way we think and live. We face a choice that is starkly simple: we must change or be changed. If we fail to change for the better, then we will be changed for the worse."[2]

Doing whatever it takes is not an act of force but an act of humility. For every man battling lust and porn, doing whatever it takes involves a step where you must trust God and trust others.

For some men this means they will share their porn struggle with someone for the very first time. For some it means having a hard conversation with their wives or girlfriends. For others it means attending a group for men struggling with porn. In some cases doing whatever it takes means getting individual counseling to explore deeper issues under the surface. In some situations men have pursued inpatient counseling, or an intensive counseling program, like the one we offer at Restoring the Soul.

We read in the gospel of John about Peter and John at the empty tomb on the first Easter morning (20:3–8). John ran ahead of Peter and arrived first—but stopped before entering. Peter arrived after him but ran straight in. God has promised you new life. Have you stepped into that new life? Standing outside the tomb won't do it.

## OUR CHANGE FOLLOWS *GOD'S* TIMELINE

In our on-demand world, we need to examine our expectations about what change and transformation look like. Transformation rarely occurs right away. If change doesn't happen according to your expectations or timetable, you'll likely get discouraged. Remember that spiritual transformation is a marathon and not a sprint.

You will inevitably experience moments—even seasons—when the power of God seems absent. More often than not, God transforms us in the mundane, everyday rhythms of life. Yes, God occasionally blesses us with "God encounters" filled with emotion and intensity. But the journey to freedom is a path of daily faithfulness. Woody Allen once said, "Eighty percent of success is just showing up." Sometimes, all you can do is show up. That's okay. On those days and seasons when not much seems to be happening, know that something *is* happening. God *is* at work: "Being confident of this, that he who began a good work in you will carry it on to completion until the day of Christ Jesus" (Phil. 1:6).

# Going Under the Knife

He looked beneath his shirt today
He saw a wound in his flesh so deep and wide
And from the wound a lovely flower grew
From somewhere deep inside
**STING, "THE LAZARUS HEART"**[1]

"Jim, you are an alcoholic," the doctor explained. This was no surprise since my father had been attending Alcoholics Anonymous for more than four years. In 1972, at the age of thirty-nine, Dad had binged on alcohol after nearly five years of continued sobriety. A blue-collar printing pressman, he had been working two full-time jobs and a part-time job. When he reached his inevitable limit, he experienced what back then was euphemistically called a "nervous breakdown." To cope, Dad returned to the bottle—the only viable option he knew at the time. A friend from AA drove him to the hospital where he began treatment. After a week of extensive mental health assessments, his psychiatrist, a straight-shooting Irishman, announced that he had reviewed the data and made a conclusive diagnosis. My father braced himself for the worst.

"Your problem is that you are immature," the doc pronounced. "You need to grow up, and learn to live without alcohol."

Dad walked back to his hospital room, where he sat for a long time to ponder the doctor's words. "I decided he was right," he told me later. "When I walked out of the room, I decided I would do whatever it took to learn to live without alcohol, to grow up." And grow up he did. Almost forty years later, he still hasn't had a drink. But even better, his journey of recovery has led him to become the man that one day I hope to be.

## BREAK UP YOUR UNPLOWED GROUND

The book of Exodus is probably best known for its portrayal of the Israelites' miraculous deliverance out of Egypt. Most of the story, however, describes the dealings of a loving God who relentlessly pursues His beloved people despite the fact that they had neither worshipped Him nor walked with Him the previous 480 years. Their previous oppression, abuse, and religious persecution turned them into a nation that no longer knew how to walk with God. Like my father who needed to face his immaturity and learn to live without alcohol, the Israelites needed to grow up and learn to live as God's free, chosen people.

During the Israelites' forty years of wandering in the desert, they repeatedly turned away from God and worshipped idols. But always faithful, God pursued them. In the book of Jeremiah, God addressed the Israelites during one of their many cycles of idolatry and disobedience. Because God's sons were engaged in spiritual and physical adultery, He used an unusual series of images filled with sexual overtones to describe His people.

> This is what the LORD says to the men of Judah and to Jerusalem:
> "Break up your unplowed ground
>     and do not sow among thorns.
> Circumcise yourselves to the LORD,
>     circumcise your hearts,
>     you men of Judah and people of Jerusalem. (Jer. 4:3–4)

God told His people to break up their unplowed ground, referring not to soil but to the ground of their hearts. The Israelites' hearts had grown hard and unreceptive, like parched land that can't absorb rainfall. The soil of their hearts had become barren and unable to grow anything. In order to yield a harvest, the fallow ground needed to be broken. Their hearts needed to be broken in order to absorb God's love.

Next, God warned the Israelites not to sow among thorns, meaning they were planting seeds in places that were unable to bring forth life. Their worship of idols was akin to planting seed in thorny ground. With their hearts unplowed and their seeds planted among thorns, their actions prevented them from giving or receiving, blessing or being blessed.

Finally, God commanded the Israelites to circumcise their hearts. But what exactly does this mean?

## CUT OFF THE FORESKIN OF YOUR HEART

Have you ever wondered what in the world cutting off the foreskin of the penis has in common with our faith in God? Wouldn't it be a whole lot easier if God asked for a lock of hair? But God instructed the men of Judah and Jerusalem to circumcise their hearts. Why circumcision?

The story of circumcision goes back to Genesis 17, when God appeared to Abram at the ripe old age of ninety-nine. By this time he and his wife, Sarai, assumed they were never going to have children. But God made a covenant with Abram that resulted in a promise, a new identity, and a command. God promised Abram that He would make him fruitful, despite not having children at the time. God gave him a new identity, changing Abram's name to Abraham (and Sarai's to Sarah). But God also commanded Abraham to circumcise every male descendent—to cut away the foreskin of the penis. Circumcision was an act of surrender to God, a way to remember God's promise, and a means of marking God's people with a new identity.

You may still be asking, *why the penis?* Why *not* the lock of hair? What was God hoping to accomplish by cutting away a man's foreskin? Circumcision represents at least three things. First, a man's penis represents his *masculine identity*, reaching beyond social and cultural definitions of manhood. It symbolizes the way a man uses his strength: to move toward others and enter their space to bless or curse, to give or take, to deposit or withdraw. In circumcision, a man surrenders his masculine identity to God. Cutting away the foreskin required a man to bear the weight of redemptive suffering.

Secondly, cutting off the foreskin of the penis represented the paring away of the *hidden self*. This hidden and private part of a man was reserved for the most intimate of relations; no one else had access to his innermost part. But God established his relationship with Israel in this most intimate of rituals. Further, ever since Adam and Eve covered themselves with fig leaves, we have mastered the art of hiding our true selves. "*I heard you in the garden, and I was afraid because I was naked; so I hid*" (Gen. 3:10). By commanding men to be circumcised, God pulled back the fig leaf of shame, requiring us to be naked—but not hide.

Finally, the foreskin and penis symbolize the *part of us that gives life*. From a reproductive slant, the penis enables us to "be fruitful and multiply" (Gen. 9:7 ESV). But a man is called to give life, to be fruitful, in areas far beyond sexual intercourse. A man has the potential to pour life into others through word and deed. Relationally, we bear a life-giving capacity to bless or curse, serve or exploit, encourage or discourage. In the depths of our masculine souls we have a capability to love or to remain indifferent, to give or to take.

Ultimately, we each decide whether we will grow up. As we

grow up, we are transformed from brokenness to wholeness, emptiness to fullness, and self-absorption to other-centeredness. The result is that we can more freely give life.

Circumcision of the heart is just as symbolic as circumcision of the flesh. Paul tells us that a man can be physically circumcised without being spiritually circumcised.

> A man is not a Jew if he is only one outwardly, nor is circumcision merely outward and physical. No, a man is a Jew if he is one inwardly; and circumcision is circumcision of the heart, by the Spirit, not by the written code. (Rom. 2:28–29)

Circumcision of the penis is an external act of surrender, remembrance, and new identity. Circumcision of the heart represents these same three realities internally. When Jesus criticized the Pharisees because they honored Him with their lips but their hearts were far from Him (Matt. 15:8), He might as well have said, "You've honored Me by surrendering your foreskin, but you haven't surrendered your heart." Going through the motions is not what God desires. He wants our external and internal selves to come into alignment.

We circumcise our hearts as a symbol of our internal love and devotion to God. A circumcised heart gives God access to our hidden selves, establishes our new identities, and offers life to others.

## WE NEED *ACCESSIBILITY* MORE THAN *ACCOUNTABILITY*

In the battle against lust and porn, most Christian approaches stress the importance of accountability. In my experience, however, what we need more than accountability is *accessibility*. During my sexual struggles, I was held accountable by friends and mentors who were among the most insightful and highly trained men around. But I

didn't have the ability or desire to let these men into my heart.
Below is an excerpt from my July 1994 journal.

> The most surprising, confounding, and tragic aspect of my actions
> is that long before I deceived anyone else, I deceived myself. For
> at least two years in our marriage, a growing, cancerous growth
> of falsehood attached itself to me. I've said all along, "That's not
> a deadly tumor, it's just a blemish." As each sexual boundary has
> been crossed, I've minimized, rationalized, excused, or done pen-
> ance. I've closed myself off to friends, telling them a fraction of
> what was really happening. I've closed myself off to God, trying
> harder to do the things I thought would please him. I'm an arro-
> gant, stubborn-hearted, self-sufficient man. Lord, I believe you
> resist the proud and give grace to the humble. Humble me. I need
> your grace and truth like never before.

When my friend Jeffrey's multiple adulterous affairs were exposed,
I asked him how I might help. He told me that what he really needed
most was an accountability relationship. Something inside me sank.
*Really?* Your marriage is dangling by a thread, and you want *accountability?* When I asked him what he had in mind, he told me he was
hoping for someone who would check in with him regarding his
"purity level." A colleague had given him a list of accountability questions. Would I meet with him every week to review them?

Jeffrey desperately needed accountability. The tragedy is that, like
many men today, his understanding of accountability was dreadfully
inadequate. Accountability is usually approached in three ways—two
common, and one less common. I call the first common approach
*cop accountability.* Our chosen accountability partner represents law
enforcement, and we are the law-abiding citizen with a proclivity for
exceeding the posted limits of appropriate sexual behavior. When we
exceed the lawful limits, we turn ourselves in to a law enforcement

officer, who issues the appropriate citation. I wish I could say that my description here is written entirely in jest, but I would be lying. With the cop accountability strategy, I believe that by sharing my sin with someone, I will have greater incentive to choose what is right. It's about the avoidance of shame. This form of accountability is a gospel of sin management that is all too common, and fraught with problems.

The most obvious issue with this approach is that every addict is a master at deception. We lie. It's what addicts do. I've lied while looking in the eyes of my wife, my best friend, and my mentor. Next, this approach relies on external reinforcement. When removed, the compulsive and addictive behaviors return. Also, this form of accountability never deals with the heart. Jesus, on the other hand, said that sexual immorality begins in the heart (Matt. 15:19). Very rarely do I hear men discussing their hearts with one another. We don't have a language for it. Finally, the man who lives under the cop accountability approach will eventually fail in one of two ways. He will suffer from a chronic sense of failing to measure up, which only serves to reinforce shameful core beliefs. Or he will succumb to pride (similar to the Pharisees of Jesus' day) resulting from his mastery of sin. Neither of these directions addresses what's actually going on. And they reinforce a gospel of sin management.

The next approach is what I call *coach accountability*. Our accountability partner plays the role of an instructor, trainer, and coach, who helps us manage our lives so we can keep moving forward. We are second-string players on God's team with a pretty good shot of making it to the spiritual big leagues. When we fail to perform well, we check in with the coach, who encourages us from the rulebook, sends us back in the game, and tells us to keep our eye on the ball. This approach implies that if we give it enough effort, time, and attention, we can earn a victory over sin and make our lives work. This "try harder" emphasis concerns itself less with sin management and more with the relentless effort to be good. It is a gospel of inspiration.

*Coach accountability* is better than *cop accountability*. At various times in our lives all of us need a friend or loved one to get in our face like a cop and say, "Stop!" In the same way, all of us periodically need encouragement, hope, and even training or equipping about how to do life. We occasionally need that coach who will come alongside us and inspire us to do our best. But ultimately we need someone to care for our hearts.

Every man needs *cardiologist accountability*. In the midst of my struggle, I lacked a safe place to talk about my brokenness. I had no language to talk about my heart and my inner world. Nobody ever asked me if lust was a struggle for me. No one ever asked me why at twenty-three years of age I had never gone on a date or had a girlfriend, or why I had a compulsive need to be funny. We need someone to ask us questions not only about our behavior but also about our hearts. We need a friend who will ask us questions about the lies we believe and help us interpret the stories that contribute to who we are today.

In the cardiologist approach we move from accountability to accessibility. We expose our hiddenness, but more than that, we acknowledge our brokenness. Instead of trying to manage our sin, or be inspired to obey, we recognize our need for transformation. We begin to allow God, and a few others, to walk into the messiness of our lives, and we learn that we are more than the sum of our brokenness.

Cardiologist accountability does not require a professional therapist or counselor. It begins with the assumption that our whole lives, including our brokenness, are the soil in which God grows us. The only requirements for becoming a cardiologist of this kind are a healthy curiosity, a desire to be a caring friend, and a willingness to grow in your understanding of the process of spiritual transformation.

## A CIRCUMCISED HEART SYMBOLIZES
## OUR NEW IDENTITIES

For the first thirty years of my life, my family and friends knew me as Mike. In 1994, after my adultery and sexual addictions were exposed, I felt a stirring inside me to be called by my given name of Michael. This choice wasn't easy at first. Suddenly going from Mike to Michael was awkward for me and my friends, but I wanted this change for several reasons. First, it signified my intention to grow up. *Mike* was the boy, the deceiver, the charmer, who refused to grow up. *Michael* felt like the part of me who was whole. I also chose my given name because it symbolized how God was calling me to take myself more seriously, to own the full weight of my soul, to run on all eight cylinders instead of four or six. But the most compelling—and most difficult—reason I chose to go by my full name was that *Michael* means "one who is like God." *Who am I to say that I'm like God?* I asked myself. But in reality, I *am* like God. *You* are like God—if you've given your heart to Him. You share His heart.

You've probably identified yourself as something less than how God identifies you. Maybe you identify yourself as shameful, worthless, inadequate, or weak. You don't think you measure up to society's expectations of a man. Maybe you base your value on your income or the neighborhood you live in. Whatever you choose to define yourself by—that is where God wants to meet you, heal you, and deliver you from these faulty and death-giving identities.

Earlier, I shared that I was twenty-three years old before I went on my first date. As I learned to flex the muscles of my masculine soul, my counselor encouraged me to take the risk of pursuing a woman romantically. When I finally mustered up the courage, I phoned a young woman and asked her specifically, "Would you like to go on a date with me to get some ice cream?" Her reply was a flat-out no. When I hung up the phone, I pumped my arm, shouted,

"YES!" and then started a victory dance. I couldn't stop laughing despite being turned down cold. It didn't matter! I just asked someone out. What was so significant about that rejection is that regardless of whether she said yes, I was living out of my identity. I was a strong man who could move toward a woman—whether she accepted me or rejected me. In that moment I became very aware that my identity was not based on whether she said yes or no.

Take a moment right now and ask yourself what you rely on to establish your identity. In light of what God's Word says about circumcision of the heart, what would it mean for you to surrender whatever defines you in order to let God define you?

## ONLY HEART SURGERY CAN HEAL US

A number of years ago, my friend Ian Cron wrote some lyrics to a song that describes this work of healing: "I own a secret I learned long ago. Love is like going under the knife. We go with great trembling and fear in our hearts. But when we wake up we find our lives."[2] If we want to grow up and learn to live without the cancer that slowly devours our souls, we must go under the knife. The surgery in our souls can only be performed by the Great Physician. And like any reputable surgeon, Jesus will not operate without our consent.

What does this surgery look like? Certainly it involves the everyday, sometimes mundane, act of following Jesus through the daily trials of life. But we also need Jesus to operate on our hidden parts, our false identities, and the areas that have turned inward and become a prison of self. Fortunately, Jesus really does heal.

God promises to set captives free and heal broken hearts (Isaiah 61:1–3). But someone once told me that in the Gospels Jesus never heals two blind men the same way. Sometimes the healing work of Jesus occurs over time, like a fractured bone that is set in a cast and then given time to fuse together. At other times, Jesus heals in an instant. Regardless of the manner in which healing occurs, the work of healing always flows from the good heart of God who seeks to restore us.

Marc was a pastor in his fifties with a flourishing church. When his wife caught him watching online porn for the third time, she courageously told him he needed to get help. On the first day that Marc participated in our soul care intensive, I instructed him to spend some time in silence, solitude, and centering prayer. On the second day, I asked him to describe his experience. He told me that his mind wandered, he thought it was a waste of time, and he questioned what the exercise had to do with his struggle with porn. I encouraged him to try again, so he did. The third day he brought me the same report. But this time I told him to begin his time of prayer by asking Jesus a simple question: "Jesus, what do You want to say to me?"

The next day when Marc walked in the door, his eyes were filled with tears, and he had a smile on his face. "What's going on?" I asked.

"You're not going to believe this," he told me. "But God spoke to me! Jesus answered my question. In fact, when I asked Him what He wanted to say to me, I heard a voice within tell me to get my journal and get ready." Immediately after retrieving his journal, he was so overcome with emotion that he laid facedown on the floor. Over the next thirty minutes, Jesus spoke these words:

*Marc, you have no idea how much I love you. My heart for you is no different now than it was when you first gave your life to Me years ago. Every time you watched porn, I was right there loving you. I am proud of you, like a father with his son. Each time you surfed for porn, I know that you were really surfing for Me. Marc, I want to heal you. Come to Me with your broken heart. I want to teach you how to hear My voice. Come. Be still and know that I am God.*

Though he preached about grace, Marc was inwardly convinced

that God was disappointed, frustrated, and fed up with him because of his sexual struggles. He had no clue that God could or would ever speak such words to him. Even more, he had no idea that such a relationship with God was possible. Each day over the course of the next two weeks, Marc took beginning steps of learning to be still in God's presence. And every day God spoke words of healing to Marc. He revealed intimate truth to counter Marc's shame-based core beliefs. He spoke words of affirmation, approval, and affection to counter the wounds from his dad's emotional absence. He spoke words of blessing and vision, assuring Marc that he had a future and a purpose in God's kingdom. In learning to be still, Marc discovered a whole new way to walk with God—a way of walking that brought real life to his soul.

The most important experience for Marc occurred toward the end of our intensive. When Marc was ten, he discovered his father's stash of *Playboy* magazines in the drawer of an old dresser in the basement. Immediately, he was hooked, and soon he discovered masturbation. From then on, several times a week, he sneaked into the basement and drank in his father's porn with a mixture of thrill and fear. One day, he went to the basement, and unknowingly witnessed his father masturbating to the porn. Each had seen the other, but Marc hurried back upstairs. He walked to his bedroom, buried his face in his pillow, and cried. The incident was never discussed.

For reasons he couldn't explain, he felt that he needed to share this memory with me. As he did, we asked Jesus together what He wanted to do with this memory. No sooner had we begun to pray than, in the eyes of his heart, Marc saw himself in the basement as a little boy. That little boy was afraid, confused, and ashamed. In my office, Marc began experiencing those same feelings.

He saw himself making a vow to never speak to anyone about what happened. Then, while reliving the experience, Jesus appeared in the basement with the little boy and asked a simple question: *Will you let Me circumcise your heart?* Marc began to chuckle at the question. The fifty-something pastor knew intellectually what this meant, but neither he nor the little boy knew what it meant practically. I encouraged Marc to ask the Great Physician what this meant.

"Jesus, what does it mean for you to circumcise my heart?" he inquired.

Graciously, Jesus responded with three more questions: *Will you give Me access to this hidden, private part of your heart? As I gain entry here, will you let Me give you a new identity—to replace your false identity that you're just like your dad? As you live in your new identity, will you let Me make you fruitful in the place of your weakness and wounding?* Without hesitation, Marc answered yes to all three of Jesus' questions. It was an absolutely beautiful, sacred moment.

When Marc completed his ten-day soul care intensive, he understood that this was not the end of his journey, but the beginning. Our time together was not about fixing him or giving him an emotional experience that would wear off shortly after getting home. Instead, it was concerned with equipping him and giving him a launching pad into a life of restoration.

This is the life that God calls each of us toward. To enter into this deeper, fuller life, however, we must learn to live without something. Like my father who needed to grow up and learn to live without alcohol. Like the Israelites who needed to grow up and learn to live freely without idols. And like Marc, who needed to grow up by learning to live without the barriers he built to keep away the shame and inadequacy.

If you are struggling with porn, it's likely that you struggle with hiddenness and false identity. And you have sought to find life apart from God. Have you circumcised your heart?

Recently, I heard a Christian expert in sexual addiction suggest that telling men to pray more in order to overcome porn was tantamount to spiritual abuse. On one level I totally agree. Any approach that does not take into account the whole person—emotional, relational, and physiological, as well as spiritual—is incomplete. To emphasize the spiritual at the expense of our total personhood is a reduced gospel.

Having said that, I invite you to pray this prayer as a way of circumcising your heart. Ask God to show you what each part means for you personally. Make it a regular part of your life.

## A PRAYER FOR CIRCUMCISING YOUR HEART

*Heavenly Father,*

*You commanded Abraham and the sons of Israel to circumcise their flesh. They chose to obey You, bearing physical pain in order to remember your covenant, and to set themselves apart for You. Knowing that a man can say and do all the right things to keep Your commands, and still have his heart far from You, You commanded the men of Judah and of Jerusalem to circumcise their hearts.*

*I come to You now to circumcise my heart. In true humility—choosing to trust You with myself, I bring my wickedness (take a moment here to confess specific sin), my weakness (take a moment here and speak out your vulnerabilities, limitations, etc.), my wounds (name them or ask God to reveal them), and the warfare brought against me (confess the lies you have believed). I offer it all to You, trusting You with it.*

*In circumcising my heart, I declare that my heart longs for more than external obedience. I announce that You have given me a new heart and put Your spirit in me so that I long to keep Your commands. I announce that when You made my heart new, You gave me the "want to's" in exchange for the "have to's." I announce that what is ultimately true about my heart is that your desires and my desires are the same.*

*In circumcising my heart I surrender my masculine identity to You. I confess all of the ways in which I have sought to define my manhood apart from You. I confess all the ways in which I have misused or abdicated my true strength as a man. Continue to show me my true identity in You, and help me grow up so I can be the man of God You created me to be.*

*In circumcising my heart I surrender the hidden parts of who I am. I confess all the ways which I have hidden my heart, my wickedness, my weakness, and my wounds. Thank You that through Jesus' death on the cross and resurrection to new life, You bring life from my brokenness. I choose now to come out of hiding and live in Your light.*

*In circumcising my heart I surrender all I am—my mind, will, emotions, spirit, and body. Thank You that through my surrendered weaknesses and wounds, You are able to bear fruit for Your kingdom. I accept Your call on my life, acknowledging that You have given me breath today to walk with You as Your beloved son.*

*In circumcising my heart I submit myself to the Lord Jesus Christ. I resist the schemes, works, and effects of the Enemy. In the authority of Jesus' name, I renounce my participation in sexual sin* (take a moment and confess specific sins such as pornography, sexual immorality, or adultery). *I demolish every sexual stronghold, and I take back any ground in my heart that has been given to the Enemy because of sexual sin.*

*Finally, in circumcising my heart I announce that it is only by the shed blood of Jesus—His death, resurrection, and ascension—that I am forgiven, cleansed, and restored to new life. Because of Jesus' life, death, and work, I announce that just as I am, I am perfectly acceptable and holy to God.*

*In the name of the Father, Son, and Holy Spirit.*
*Amen.*

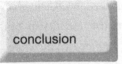

# Becoming the Hero That You Are

God made men the way they are because we
desperately need them to be the way they are.

**—JOHN ELDREDGE**[1]

Let's return for a moment to our story of the rabbi and the student . . .

A rabbi and his young disciple sat side by side under the shade of a large oak tree.

"Help me, Rabbi," said the disciple. "I am a double-minded man. The law of the Lord tells me, 'The Lord is my Shepherd and I shall not be in want.' But oh, how I want!"

You remember the story. The disciple poured out his soul—all of his secret sin and shame—to his rabbi. But this time, the story has a different ending.

"My son," began the rabbi. "Listen to the story I am about to tell you.

"Long ago, when I was quite young, I asked *my* rabbi to explain a passage that I never understood.

"'In the book of Genesis, the story is told that after Adam bit into the fruit, he hid from God. Is that correct?' I asked my teacher.

"'That is correct,' he said.

"'And is it correct that after Adam fled, God asked him, "Where are you?"'

"'That is correct,' my teacher answered.

"'Then how is it conceivable that the Creator of the universe did not know where Adam was hiding?'

"'The Lord knew where Adam was,' said my teacher. 'It was Adam who did not know.'"[2]

## WHERE ARE YOU?

God knows exactly where you are. But do *you* know where you are? If you do, that is your starting point. Your journey begins right where you are, not where you ought to be. Are you lost? If so, it's perfectly okay to stop and ask for directions. Acknowledging you are lost is a condition for completing the journey. Jesus is a trustworthy guide. So where are *you* in:

- understanding the root issues as to why you struggle with porn?
- recognizing the empty promises porn has made to you and knowing your God-given desires for which porn is a substitute?
- owning your personal brokenness and resisting shame's grip on your soul?
- uncovering the lies you believe and living out of your good heart?
- learning how to care for your own soul?

## A VISION FOR YOUR LIFE

My friend Victor has struggled with porn addiction for decades. At this stage of our lives, we only see each other occasionally. But whenever he sees me, he always calls me his hero. At first this was embarrassing and awkward. But each time he saw me, he explained that my story of redemption gave him hope that he, too, could be free.

After two years without seeing Victor, I ran into him at a going-away party for some mutual friends. At first I didn't recognize him. His monotone voice was now infused with energy. His once-constrained personality was more vibrant and animated. His eyes were bright and clear. He even seemed more physically fit. I had never seen Victor exuding such joy.

"What *happened* to you?" I asked.

"Michael, I'm free," he said. "And if it can happen to me, it can happen to anyone."

You can imagine how curious I was to know more about his transformation. This is what he said:

"Since junior high I've fought a war against lust and porn. I finally got tired of putting so much energy into battling porn, so I gave up. Instead, I've been putting my energy into becoming a different kind of man. I'm changing the way I do life. I'm starting to see myself and God differently. I'm learning what intimacy is all about. I guess I'm becoming a man who just doesn't need to look at porn anymore. What it once did for me, I no longer need, because the gaping hole in my heart is gone. I'm pursuing God for who He is and not what He can do for me. I'm focusing on being transformed and discovering that it's actually starting to happen."

"A hero," wrote Joseph Campbell, "is someone who has given his life to something bigger than himself."[3] Today Victor is *my* hero.

## SLAYING THE LIZARD

In his allegory *The Great Divorce*, C. S. Lewis described a world where no one needs God, or anyone else, for that matter. That place is hell. People can get whatever they want simply by imagining it, although what they receive isn't real (reminiscent of porn).

In one scene the ghost of a man is enslaved to lust. A red lizard—the symbol for his lust—sits upon the man's shoulder and constantly whispers lies in his ear. As the man becomes more and more distressed, an angel appears and offers to kill the lizard. But the ghost-man is torn. He doesn't want the lizard anymore, but he doesn't want it to die, out of fear that he, too, will die. So, he offers excuses to the angel. "I don't want to bother you . . . Let's not kill it; let's just silence it . . . There is not enough time . . . It's sleeping now and won't bother me . . . Let me talk to someone who knows more about this kind of thing to see if this is necessary."

The angel patiently counters each excuse by asking permission to kill the lizard. In one last attempt at avoiding the necessary pain, the ghost launches a verbal assault against the angel. "If you wanted to help me, why didn't you kill the damned thing without asking me—before I knew? It would be all over now if you had." But the angel replies, "I cannot kill it against your will. It is impossible. Have I your permission?" Finally, the ghost-man relents and the angel proceeds to break the back of the lizard of lust, throwing it dead on the ground.

What happens next in this story is utterly beautiful. The ghost-man, once formless and without substance, begins taking shape and adding weight. First an arm, then a shoulder, and then legs and hands. Next a neck and head, until he transforms into a complete man, gloriously radiant and solid. Unexpectedly, the lizard, too, begins changing size and shape. Slowly, it morphs from a scaly-red reptile into a silvery-white stallion. Its tail and mane are made of gold, and its muscles ripple as it whinnies and stamps its hooves. When the newly made solid-man sees the stallion, he hops on its back and heads off toward the mountains.[4]

Like the ghost-man in Lewis's story, lust is never far away. It sits on men's shoulders and whispers lies. It tries to entice them to believe that it will give them what they want and need. That it will satisfy their deep thirsts and heal their brokenness. It has enticed you too. Lust seeks to seduce you into surrendering your heart. And when you give in, at some level, your brain, your behavior, and your soul become ensnared. This is not who you wanted to be.

And this is not who you are. Not ultimately.

It's very likely that you identify more with the red lizard of lust in Lewis's story than the white stallion. But you must understand the truth. Right now you *are* that white stallion. You *are* that complete man. Beneath your brokenness, your strong, masculine heart remains intact. You are noble. You are honorable. You are a hero. And your strength is desperately needed.

God longs to transform your lust into strength. It won't happen, however, through more religious effort. It won't happen by recruiting one more accountability partner. It won't even happen just by reading this book and deciding that *this* time you're going to be more serious about avoiding temptation.

Today you face a choice. You can minimize the impact of porn on your soul and life. You can blame others to justify your sexual sin. You can stay hidden, ruled by brokenness. You can continue trying harder to do better until you give up from exhaustion. And you can settle for only *dreaming* of holiness and freedom, pouring life into those you love and the world around you.

Or you can choose life. Choosing life, which is easier said than done, is the path you must walk in order for your soul to be free. Choosing life means believing you are a stallion. That you were created to fly and sing the song in your heart. Choosing life means acknowledging that the road you have been traveling leads to death. That on a behavioral level you have been surfing for porn, while on a heart level you have been surfing for God. And most important, choosing life means believing that your heavenly Father has a better way of doing your life than you.

God faithfully pursued Adam, even as he disobeyed, hid, and lost his bearings. And God is faithfully pursuing you.

Where are *you*?

## acknowledgments

My sincere thanks to: Dudley Delffs—friend, brother, literary agent; Michael J. Klassen—substantive editorial contributor; Judy Gomoll—encourager, friend, editor. Special thanks to the team at Thomas Nelson: Renee Chavez, Adria Haley, and Matt Baugher.

Deep gratitude to Cleveland Young Life, the men who poured into my life and set the bar so high: Jeff Coakwell, Joel LaRiccia, Don Mook, and John Bush. Thanks to Dr. Michael Misja of North Coast Family Foundation—the first person to fight for my heart.

I am indebted to Dan Allender and Tom Varney, who taught and mentored me in counseling and caring for souls. To John Eldredge, who points me to Jesus. I am especially grateful to Larry Crabb, who blazed a path for all of us by offering fresh truth about sanctification and holiness, and who guided Julianne and me through the valley and into the light.

My heartfelt appreciation goes out to Bill and Laurie Bolthouse, Kim and Michelle Hutchins, Al and Nita Andrews, Philip Yancey, John and Elaine Busch, Aram Haroutunian, Eric Ebeling, Brad and Jeanette Hillman, Patty Wolf, Denise Simpson, and Steve Siler. Thanks to Gary Wilson for critical input regarding "Your Brain on Porn"—simplifying the wonder of the brain. Special thanks to Chris and Katinka Bryson, Kathy and Tom Norman, Dick and Bo Teodoro, Billy Williams, and Peter Zaremba for making my writing sabbatical a reality.

## ACKNOWLEDGMENTS

David and Faith Donaldson: All the king's horses and all the king's men couldn't put Humpty Dumpty back together, but you were the King's hands and heart in putting me back together. Bless you.

Lily Mei, CJ, and Julianne—you have my heart, filled with joy for our life together.

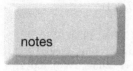
notes

## Introduction: What's Better than Porn?

1. I first heard this story in the 1980s as a sermon illustration. In 2001 I read it in Jeffrey Satinover's book *Feathers of the Skylark: Compulsion, Sin and Our Need for a Messiah*. Although I have adapted it here by creating the character of the rabbi, the original story is probably attributable to G. H. Charnley, a British minister. See G. H. Charnley, *Skylark's Bargain: Thirty-Seven Talks to Boys and Girls* (London: H. R. Allenson Publisher, 1920).

## Chapter 1: Getting Your Feathers Back

1. Gerald May, *Addiction and Grace: Love and Spirituality in the Healing of Addictions* (New York: HarperCollins, 1998).
2. From personal correspondence by C. S. Lewis, in the Wade [Private] Collection at Wheaton College, Wheaton, IL.
3. Ibid.
4. Augustine had some biblically unfounded ideas about sex, including the notion that sex was only for procreation.
5. Donald Miller, *A Million Miles in a Thousand Years: What I Learned While Editing My Life* (Nashville: Thomas Nelson, 2009), 198.

## Chapter 2: It's Not About Sex

1. Oswald Chambers, *The Philosophy of Sin: How to Deal with Moral Problems* (London: Marshall, Morgan, & Scott, 1960).
2. John Eldredge, *Wild at Heart: Discovering the Secret of a Man's Soul* (Nashville: Thomas Nelson, 2001), 44.
3. Robert Jensen, *Getting Off: Pornography and the End of Masculinity* (Cambridge, MA: South End Press, 2007), 33.
4. C. S. Lewis, *The Four Loves* (Orlando: Harcourt, Brace, 1960), 121.
5. *American Beauty*, Dreamworks/SKG, 1999.

## Chapter 3: Insatiable Thirst

1. David A. Bender, *Encyclopedia.com*, s.v., "aposia," http://www.encyclopedia.com/doc/1O39-aposia.html, accessed October 17, 2011.
2. Eldredge, *Wild at Heart*, 201.
3. Frederick Buechner, *Godric* (New York: HarperCollins, 1980), 153.
4. C. S. Lewis, *The Weight of Glory* (New York: HarperCollins, 1949), 1.
5. C. S. Lewis, *The Great Divorce* (New York: HarperCollins, 1946), 106–11.
6. Larry Crabb, *Inside Out* (Colorado Springs: NavPress, 2007), 105.

## Chapter 4: Gathering the Broken Pieces

1. Richard Rohr, *On the Threshold of Transformation: Daily Meditations for Men* (Chicago: Loyola Press, 2010), 98.
2. Crabb, *Inside Out*, 49.
3. D. H. Lawrence, in *D. H. Lawrence: Selected Poetry*, Keith Sagar, ed., rev. ed. (London: Penguin, 1989), 216–17.
4. Richard Rohr, *Daily Meditations for Men* (Chicago: Loyola Press, 2010), 48.
5. Sam Keen, *To a Dancing God* (New York: Harper & Row, 1970). Quoted at http://www.inwardoutward.org/autho/sam-keen.

## Chapter 5: Exposing the Counterfeits

1. Quoted in John Eldredge, *The Journey of Desire: Searching for the Life We've Only Dreamed Of* (Nashville: Thomas Nelson, 2000), 80.
2. Fyodor Dostoyevsky, *The Brothers Karamazov* (New York: Random House, 1990), 394.
3. Tim Keller, *Counterfeit Gods: The Empty Promises of Money, Sex, Power, and the Only Hope That Matters* (New York: Dutton, 2009), xvii.
4. A. W. Tozer, *The Knowledge of the Holy* (San Francisco: Harper, 1961), 6.
5. Keller, *Counterfeit Gods*, xvii.
6. Ibid., 155.

## Chapter 6: Shame and Core Beliefs

1. Bruce Springsteen, "Better Days," on Bruce Springsteen's *Human Touch* (album), produced by Chuck Plotkin, Jon Landau, 1992.
2. Andrew Comiskey, *Strength in Weakness: Healing Sexual and Relational Brokenness* (Downers Grove, IL: IVP Books, 2003), 69.
3. Alan Paton, *Too Late the Phalarope* (New York: Scribners, 1953), 3.
4. Patrick Carnes, *Out of the Shadows: Understanding Sexual Addiction* (Center City, MN: Hazleden Press, 1983), 167–76.
5. Henri Nouwen, *Life of the Beloved: Spiritual Living in a Secular World* (New York: Crossroads Publishing, 1992), 33.

6. Thomas Merton, Inward/Outward website, http://www.inwardoutward.org/author/thomas-merton?page=1.

## Chapter 7: The Soul Snare Path

1. Gordon Dalbey, *Fight Like a Man* (Carol Stream, IL: Tyndale House, 1995).
2. http://www.brainyquote.com/quotes/quotes/carljung114799.html.
3. May, *Addiction and Grace*, 29.
4. John Donne, Sonnet 14 from *Poems of John Donne*, vol. 1, E. K. Chambers, ed. (London: Lawrence and Vullen, 1896), 165.

## Chapter 8: Your Good Heart

1. Gerald May, *The Awakened Heart* (New York: HarperCollins, 1991).
2. Michael John Cusick, "A Conversation with Dallas Willard," http://www.restoringthesoul.com/interviews.

## Chapter 9: The Invisible Battle

1. Philip Yancey, *A Skeptic's Guide to Faith* (Grand Rapids: Zondervan, 2003), 92.
2. Christopher West, *Theology of the Body for Beginners* (West Chester, PA: Ascension Press, 2004), 11.
3. Calvin Miller, *Disarming the Darkness: A Guide to Spiritual Warfare* (Grand Rapids: Zondervan, 1998), 62–63.
4. This prayer was originally published in *Love & War* by John and Stasi Eldredge, who graciously gave permission for it to be used here. You can download a copy of the prayer at http://www.ransomedheart.com/more_prayers.aspx.

## Chapter 10: Your Brain on Porn

1. Sharon Begley, *Train Your Mind, Change Your Brain: How a New Science Reveals Our Extraordinary Potential to Transform Ourselves* (New York: Ballantine Books, 2007), 9.
2. U2, Brian Eno, and Daniel Lanois, "Unknown Caller," on U2's *No Line on the Horizon* (album), produced by Brian Eno, Daniel Lanois, and Steve Lillywhite, 2009.
3. Partnership for a Drug-Free America, "Brain on Drugs" (public service announcement), viewable on YouTube at http://www.youtube.com/watch?v=dk9XY8Nrs0A&feature=related.
4. American Society of Addiction Medicine, Public Policy Statement, Definition of Addiction, August 15, 2011, http://www.asam.org/About.html.
5. Mary Sykes Wylie and Richard Simon, *Psychotherapy Networker*, September 1, 2002. The entire article is available at http://www.highbeam.com/doc/1P3-671613861.html.

6. Marnia Robinson, "Sex and Morality: A Debate Between Competing Neurons," published on January 12, 2011, in Cupid's Poisoned Arrow, http://www.psychologytoday.com/blog/cupids-poisoned-arrow/201101/sex-and-morality-debate-between-competing-neurons.

7. Gary Wilson describes this on his website, www.yourbrainonporn.com.

8. Norman Doidge, *The Brain That Changes Itself: Stories of Personal Triumph from the Frontiers of Brain Science* (New York: Penguin, 2007), 106.

9. Gert Holstege et al., "Brain Activation During Human Male Ejaculation," *The Journal of Neuroscience* (October 8, 2003), 23(27):9185–93.

10. See *Wikipedia*, s.v., "Coolidge effect," http://en.wikipedia.org/wiki/Coolidge_effect.

11. C. S. Lewis, *The Screwtape Letters* (New York: HarperCollins, 1946), 106–11.

12. John Medina, *Brain Rules: 12 Principles for Surviving and Thriving at Work, Home, and School* (Seattle: Pear Press, 2008).

13. Marta G. Vucckovic et al., "Exercise elevates dopamine D2 receptor in a mouse model of Parkinson's disease in vivo imaging with (18F) fallypride (2010)," *Movement Disorders*, vol. 25, issue 16, 2777–84, 15 December 2010.

14. Chen Hsiun Ing, et al., "Long term compulsive exercise reduces the rewarding efficacy of 3,4-methylenedioxymethamphetamine," *Behav Brain Res.*, 2008 Feb 11;187(1):185–9. Epub 2007 Sep 16.

15. I am grateful to Gary Wilson for allowing me to liberally draw from his collected research and simplified scientific explanations. His website http://yourbrainonporn.com is an invaluable resource.

## Chapter 11: Less Is More

1. Isa. 30:15.

2. Adam Duritz, "Perfect Blue Buildings," on Counting Crows' *August and Everything After* (album), produced by T-Bone Burnett, 1993.

3. Henri J. M. Nouwen, *Reaching Out: Three Movements of the Spiritual Life* (New York: Doubleday, 1975), 18.

4. Keller, *Counterfeit Gods*, 155.

5. Henri Nouwen, *Making All Things New: An Invitation to the Spiritual Life* (New York: HarperCollins, 1981), 70.

6. Mirabai Starr, transl. in *The Interior Castle: St. Teresa of Avila* (Riverhead Books, 2003), 3.

7. Brother Lawrence, *Practicing the Presence of God* (Brewster, MA: Paraclete Press, 2007).

8. David Muyskens, *Forty Days to a Closer Walk with God* (Nashville: Upper Room, 2006).

9. Mindfulness meditation is "a kind of nonelaborative, nonjudgmental, present-centered awareness in which each thought, feeling, or sensation that arises in the attentional field is acknowledged and accepted as it is." Scott R. Bishop et al., "Mindfulness: A proposed operational definition,"

*Clinical Psychology: Science and Practice* 11, no. 3 (2004): 232; see also 230–41.

10. Ruth A. Baer, "Mindfulness training as a clinical intervention: A conceptual and empirical review," *Clinical Psychology: Science and Practice* 10, no. 2 (2003): 125–43.

11. *Mindfulness for Addiction Problems* (DVD), with G. Alan Marlatt, PhD, ISBN: 978-1-59147-221-6, November 2004; K. Witkiewitz, G. A. Marlatt, and D. D. Walker, "Mindfulness-based relapse prevention for alcohol use disorders: The meditative tortoise wins the race," *Journal of Cognitive Psychotherapy* 19 (2005): 211–30.

12. Doidge, *The Brain That Changes Itself.*

## Chapter 12: The Soul Care Highway

1. Martin Nystrom, "As the Deer," 1984.

2. Ronald Rollheiser, *The Holy Longing* (New York: Doubleday, 1999), 221.

3. Peter Scazzero, *Emotionally Healthy Spirituality* (Nashville: Thomas Nelson, 2006).

## Chapter 13: Freedom to Live

1. Henri Nouwen, *In the Name of Jesus: Reflections on Christian Leadership* (New York: Crossroad Publishing, 1992).

2. Wendell Berry, *Sex, Economy, Freedom, and Community: Eight Essays* (New York: HarperCollins, 1946), 107–14.

## Chapter 14: Going Under the Knife

1. Sting, "The Lazarus Heart," on Sting's *Nothing Like the Sun* (album), produced by Neil Dorfsman, 1991.

2. Ian Morgan Cron, "All the Things That Love Can Do," on Ian Morgan Cron's *Land of My Father's* (album), produced by Rob Mathes, 1994.

## Conclusion: Becoming the Hero That You Are

1. John Eldredge, *Wild at Heart: Discovering the Secret of a Man's Soul* (Nashville: Thomas Nelson, 2001), 83.

2. I have adapted this story from a parable written in Elie Wiesel's *And the Sea Is Never Full: Memoirs, 1969—* (New York: Schocken Books, 1999), 1.

3. http://www.brainyquote.com/quotes/quotes/j/josephcamp1.

4. Lewis, *The Great Divorce*, 106–14.

# WHERE DO YOU GO FROM HERE?

Michael John Cusick is Founder and President of Restoring the Soul, a ministry that provides life-changing soul care to Christian leaders, and to the organizations in which they serve. Michael and his staff offer a number of ministry programs which take the *Surfing for God* message and help you apply its power in your life, marriage, or ministry. If you liked the book, *Surfing for God*, then consider one of the opportunities below.

- Intensive Counseling in Colorado
  (For Couples and Individuals)
- *Surfing for God* Workshops for Men
  (Group Experience in Colorado)
- *Surfing for God* Workshops for Spouses
  (Group Experience in Colroado)
- Bring Michael to your church or organization

### Find More resources at

www.surfingforgodbook.com
www.restoringthesoul.com
www.michaeljohncusick.com

**App Store for iPhone/iPad: "Surfing for God"**